PRAISE FOR

Beauty in the Wreckage

"What Brandon has done here, with so much vibrancy and passion, is guide sincere seekers through the trauma and into the sacred space of shalom to rediscover intimate love and union with God, which then moves out into our relationships and communities in wholeness and holiness."

FATHER RICHARD ROHR
FRANCISCAN AUTHOR AND TEACHER, FOUNDER OF
THE CENTER FOR ACTION AND CONTEMPLATION
IN ALBUQUERQUE, NEW MEXICO

"While it feels like our world is falling apart, where does that leave us? Where is our hope? In his book, Andress flips our fear-based framework for life on its head, reminding us that there is healing, vibrancy, transformation, and even God, in the midst of our pain. We do not need to escape our lives to find ourselves alive, to begin to mend our hurting hearts; we can find our renewal begins right where we are."

HILLARY L MCBRIDE, MA, RCC, PHD CANDIDATE
AUTHOR, THERAPIST AND CO-HOST OF THE
LITURGISTS AND OTHER PEOPLE'S PROBLEMS

"The Gospel that Jesus gave us is beautiful. But is it practical? What about when people we love die, or when our children suffer? What about when we feel alone, unloved, and unwelcome? Is the Gospel any good to us during those dark seasons of the soul? This is exactly what this book dares to explore. As you might imagine, it's not an easy path to navigate. But Brandon Andress walks us through the very real, and painful journey of real-life suffering to show us just how relevant, and necessary, the Gospel of Jesus really is for those who experience doubt, pain, fear and loneliness. This is a book for real people, with real questions, and real emotions. Brandon doesn't hold anything back, and that's why it's such a necessary book for those of us who know what it's like to wrestle with God in the dark, wondering if joy really does come with the morning sunrise. Highly recommended."

KEITH GILES

AUTHOR OF *JESUS UNBOUND: LIBERATING THE WORD OF GOD FROM THE BIBLE*

"Hope. Radical hope. Grounded hope. That's what Brandon Andress offers us wind-tossed, war-torn, beleaguered people who hunger to know that the "immeasurably more" God offers is real, relevant, for now. Important and timely, *Beauty in the Wreckage* is part battle-cry, part roadmap, part manifesto for those of us whose souls cry out "This is not all there is, and we will fight for the side of Love. We will lean in, push forward, and dwell in the eternal shalom." We need Brandon's voice and message of hope. I'm thrilled we have it."

CARY UMHAU

AUTHOR OF *BURNING DOWN THE FIREPROOF HOTEL*, CREATIVE DIRECTOR OF SPACIOUS

"Every generation needs a voice "crying out in the wilderness," calling us back to the Real when we allow the uncertainty, doubt, and chaos of our cultural climate to overwhelm us. We need a voice to call us back to what is of Ultimate Concern. We need a voice that calls us out of religiosity and back to Life. We need a voice that calls us out of the myopathy of the institutional church and back to a new way of Being in and for the world. Brandon is that voice. The call is a return to seeking fullness of Life found in following the way of Jesus. We live in increasingly contentious and divided and uncertain times. *Beauty in the Wreckage* is a call to see and experience the world differently, and that beauty, joy, and the shalom of God are possible right here and right now."

MATT POLLEY
HOST OF THE INGLORIOUS PASTERDS PODCAST

"When you're constantly bombarded with negativity, anger, and what appears to be a never-ending hopeless news cycle, it is easy to feel drained and void of life. So many of us were raised to believe that life was to be found in "setting our eyes on heaven," but what many found was that the promise of heaven did little to reduce our feelings of lifelessness and hopelessness. In a time when the Church has utterly failed to proclaim life in the here and now, Brandon has written a book that seeks to lead us back to the radical notion that living in the way of Jesus actually transforms us TODAY. Let this book wash over you like a cool breeze on a hot summer day."

BRAD POLLEY
HOST OF THE INGLORIOUS PASTERDS PODCAST

"*Beauty in the Wreckage* is insightful, thought-provoking, and transformational. This book is for those who are in the church questioning and those who have left the church because of their questions. The Kingdom of Heaven has long been the focus of the afterlife and extremely exclusive in nature. In this book, Brandon brings the Kingdom into the here and now and opens us to the reality that it is for everyone. This book sends you on a journey that shifts your focus from frustration and bitterness to being present and finding deeper meaning, beauty, and shalom."

MICHAEL BAYSINGER
HOST OF THE INGLORIOUS PASTERDS PODCAST

"*Beauty in the Wreckage* is a book that will undoubtedly change the heart of every reader. In our current culture of pain, sadness, turmoil, and anger—heartache seems to be the new normal. We don't know what to do with our pain, so we muddle through life ignoring deep wounds, numbing, blaming God, and ultimately losing hope. Brandon walks with each reader on a journey toward healing and helps us see that even in the midst of our darkest days there is a different way to see things. This book has a completely new approach that doesn't dismiss the pain and suffering, but embraces it. Brandon helps the reader see that in our brokenness and wrecked lives that there is true freedom in Christ, no matter the source of pain. Readers desperate for the full life Jesus offers will walk with Brandon towards healing, hope, and learn to truly see the beauty all around us, even among the wreckage."

SARAH DISMORE
HOST OF OUTSIDE THE WALLS PODCAST

"The world feels more polarized and cranky than ever. Rather than approaching our differences with compassion and understanding, fear has convinced us to demonize those we disagree with. In a world torn by hostility and outrage, Brandon Andress reminds us it doesn't have to be this way. In *Beauty in the Wreckage*, Andress calls us to the work of finding and sharing the peace of the Divine. May the message of this book permeate our hearts and relationships and transform the world around us."

STEVE AUSTIN
AUTHOR OF FROM *PASTOR TO A PSYCH WARD* AND *CATCHING YOUR BREATH*

First Edition

Cover design and layout by Rafael Polendo (polendo.net)

New International Version®, NIV®. Copyright ©1973, 1978, 1984, 2011 by Biblica, Inc.™ Used by permission of Zondervan. All rights reserved worldwide. www.zondervan.com The "NIV" and "New International Version" are trademarks registered in the United States Patent and Trademark Office by Biblica, Inc.™

Holy Bible: The New King James Version. 1982. Nashville: Thomas Nelson. As found in the Logos Bible study software program.

The Holy Bible: The Amplified Bible. 1987. La Habra, CA: The Lockman Foundation. As found in the Logos Bible study software program.

Holy Bible: The Message (the Bible in contemporary language). 2005. Colorado Springs, CO: NavPress. As found in the Logos Bible study software program.

ISBN 978-1-938480-36-2

This volume is printed on acid free paper and meets ANSI Z39.48 standards.

Printed in the United States of America

Published by Quoir
Orange, California

www.quoir.com

Beauty IN THE Wreckage

FINDING PEACE IN THE AGE OF OUTRAGE

BRANDON ANDRESS

Dedication

Dedicated to Abbott Forrester Garn,
Oliver Sze, and Jennifer Phelps.

We hold each of you in hope, carrying you
with us, until we are reunited.

Acknowledgements

Special thanks to Herb Haile for reading and rereading and rereading every draft, every email, and every late-night text that went into the development of this book.

Table of Contents

Foreword

There is a movement afoot of folks who are embracing the radical news that Jesus is Lord and Caesar isn't.

For too long, the history of the church has been marred by violence and compromise for the sake of power and comfort. Today, although few churches engage in holy wars, the rhetorical wars rage on. Christianity is broken in some ways, but not irredeemable.

Beyond the infighting between people of faith, we all have trials that we must face this side of the renewed creation. The way of Jesus shows us that beauty is always possible, even when the path involves the wreckage of life.

Relationships break. Circumstances break us.

Yet God's beauty, if we learn to see it, can resurrect hope and bring us to personal and communal wholeness.

Our world is fragmented and few would argue against this. We have become "I" in the West and the trend toward "we" is mediated mostly by a screen. The "we" of social media is disembodied, yet also a telltale sign of our desire to be with others. Positively, it evidences that we long for deeper relationships. And yet, this medium has created political tribalism and has pushed people further apart. Unfortunately, this version of "we" fragments in new ways as soundbite newsfeeds and vitriolic comment threads that push us even further apart. The relatives we used to *love* and *like*, well—let's just say that we still *love* them.

But this interpersonal fragmentation is only part of the problem.

The world is a mess.

Violence, disease, poverty, xenophobia, racism, and every form of exclusion tempt us daily to give up on the whole project of a better life and a better world. We see brokenness at global, national, and local levels of society and empathy overload leaves us stuck. And with divisions becoming more pronounced, we are quickly narrowing our sources of information and identity.

Who will guide us out of the chaos?

Who will assure us that we are on the "right" side of history?

Which tribe will fill this void?

These questions reveal that fear is driving us more than anything else. And most of us believe that we need these divisions to create a sense of safety and belonging. But there has to be something better.

The beauty in all of this wreckage is that God knows exactly who we truly are and exactly what we all desire. It is summed up in one biblical word…*shalom* (peace, wholeness, and harmonious relationships).

Shalom is what we all long for even if we've never picked up a Bible or gone to church. There's this sense that we're all tired of not knowing the innermost parts of our souls. We are tired of half truths. We don't actually want to segment from one another, but fear enslaves us to our tendencies toward marking out the world as spaces of "in" and "out."

Thus, polarities are perpetuated.

Shalom remains in an ongoing state of disruption.

However, followers of Jesus embrace the irrational idea that the world, as it is, isn't the world that it will be one day. The hope that followers of Christ have is that God's good world, although presently victim to the wreckage of Sin and Death, will be *liberated from its bondage to decay* (to borrow a phrase from Paul the Apostle). That is the great vision of new creation that runs through the biblical storyline from Genesis to Revelation. Jesus will bring heaven down to earth to heal, purge, and restore it for eternity. But right now, we inhabit *the world as it is*. We need to own that, perhaps more than many Christians have in previous generations.

I grew up in a context where the future was the reason for living. Regrettably, instead of the renewal of the cosmos (Romans 8, Revelation 21-22, etc.) as the ultimate future, we had some weird *Left Behind* scenarios that reinforced a wrecked narrative: this world is doomed, so escaping it is where are imaginations should lie. But lie they did (get it?) as the story of Christianity slightly morphed into earth becoming a waiting room for a detached, spiritual place called *heaven*.

But this lie, unintentional as it is for those who teach such things, has ramifications.

So does the biblical alternative of new creation. If we understand that the future intent for this world is to be a place where the fullness of God's shalom is actualized, and if we understand that part of shalom is the healing of fragmentation, then perhaps it makes sense that the New Testament continuously reminds us that these future gifts can show up in our lives today.

And that is where the Christian hope for shalom begins. It is at the intersection of *the world as it is*—and *the world as it will be*— and Jesus shows us how to find wholeness and abundant life in that place. I would go so far as to say that it is in the wreckage of life where God purges us in preparation for a better world.

But while God never causes the wreckage, God desires nothing more than to redeem it in our lives.

However, that would be too individualistic on its own.

In this same web of Sin and Death, the Spirit of God empowers us through our pain to be a collective sign of hope to our divided culture. Here and now, Christian communities can be whole and show others that the wreckage from fragmentation doesn't have to define us or be our identity.

Perhaps this all sounds a bit theoretical. Maybe a tad abstract. Well, it isn't. Each of us have endured the pain of loss or rejection at some point in our journey, some more severe than others. But, the one thing that unites us as humans in *the world as it is…* is the wreckage itself.

In *Beauty in the Wreckage,* Brandon does a fantastic job showing us that there is, in fact, beauty to be revealed in those situations. He contends that the struggle we have is learning to *see* with a new set of lenses so that we can *be* different within the spaces we inhabit. But let me be utterly clear. This isn't a book that explains the wreckage away as God's ultimate will, or as though God's plan for your life is pain. Not at all. Brandon explains that God uses the wreckage, but never causes it or condones it. In fact, God subverts it.

And in this book, we get an invitation to see the subverting influence of God in the challenges facing us today. Brandon demonstrates that suffering is a passageway to transformation, which refines us to see the resurrection beauty in spite of the brokenness. He then takes us to a place where we can see this Divine subversion of fragmentation, where we are not only invited to journey inwardly, but more deeply in intimate community with others, to discover the shalom-shaped person that God created us to be. Transformation of this sort opens our hearts and minds to feel the full wrath of the wreckage, while simultaneously experiencing counterintuitive joy and presence.

We can be whole, even if the wreckage eventually kills us.

The wholeness that we desire personally is what the world needs. As we, together, become whole, we can *be* different within the world's pain. Our prayerfully propelled and shalom redefined lives will look more and more like Jesus. Brandon, like a wise guide who has traveled the trail before us, guides readers to engage the wreckage with new lenses and resources. This is a book that invites readers to hope deeply and to lead others to healing waters of counterintuitive love.

As you read the pages that follow, I invite you to let others in on the journey. Discuss what you are learning about God and yourself. This will not be a quick fix sort of resource, but a guide for an ongoing journey of transformation. The Jesus that taught us things like "love your enemies" and "pray for those who harass you" is inviting us to become the kind of people who are no longer marked by the fragmented forces of culture, but by the mark of self-sacrificial love. And this kind of beauty may involve immense risk, but imagine a life where you become a signpost for others to see that resurrection is all around us.

Yes, even in the wreckage, shalom-shaped beauty emerges. And it begins by learning to *see* differently and then by becoming a different kind of person in the world- one who reminds others that the primary disposition of God, revealed in Jesus, has always been goodness and love.

Kurt Willems

Lead Pastor at Pangea Church in Seattle, Washington,
Writer and Podcaster at TheologyCurator.com,
and Blogger at Patheos.com

Introduction

As I took Aberdeen outside for the last time on that frigid Wednesday night in late January, I stood on the cold, dark patio and sobbed as I watched him feebly sniff the ground around him. In that moment, he was a frail, sad shadow of his former self, but also the embodiment of eighteen and a half years of profound joy, undying loyalty, and unending friendship.

And while I knew I would be sad, I didn't expect to be so heartbroken.

We were newlyweds when we bought our Miniature Schnauzer for $350 in 1998. As naïve early 20-somethings, who didn't make much money, we overdrafted our checking account that month. But in our minds, Aberdeen was going to be our trial run at having a baby. We learned the responsibility of cleaning up his messes, fixing everything he tore up, and taking him outside in the middle of the night to do his business. Aberdeen was certainly one of our children. And even leading up to his final day, we still referred to him as our first-born.

There's no question that he was the greatest overdraft we ever made.

It's hard to explain the distance between your head and your heart. Your head can be so logical, so rational, so calculated, and sometimes so detached from your heart and emotions. While Aberdeen had been slowly deteriorating over the last couple of years, we knew the time would soon be approaching when we would have to make the difficult decision. We thought that even though we would be sad from his passing, it would be made easier by the fact that he was old, losing weight, and suffering from a neurological disorder that made walking and standing difficult, and sometimes impossible.

Our heads told us that this was the right decision, but nothing told our hearts to prepare for being wrecked.

As we stood with Aberdeen in those final moments in the tiny, square examination room lit by the harsh fluorescent lights above, a flood of grief washed over us. All I could think of were the words of our oldest daughter Anna, when she said the night before, "Do you know why Aberdeen has lived so long? Because he is happy." The joy of knowing our precious dog loved us, always wanted to be with us, and was still pressing on to live another day while his little body wasted away was met with the violent and horrific tension of our inner grief as we watched him take his final breath.

All I could say with tears streaming down my face was, "I'm sorry Aberdeen. I'm so sorry."

If you have ever had a pet become a part of your family, you know how incredibly difficult that moment is. But by comparison, his passing seemed so insignificant in relation to what we had just walked through before, and then immediately after, Aberdeen's death.

A few months prior, we experienced the unforeseen loss of our close friend's newborn son, Oliver. He was a healthy full-term baby, who inexplicably died just before delivery. Neither Kim nor Wilfred, Oliver's mom and dad, nor anyone else, could have ever imagined such a horrifically painful ending to such a perfect pregnancy. And when I received Kim's dreadful text early the next morning, while I was getting ready for work, my heart felt like a cold, dark, infinite void. He was a beautiful baby boy whom neither Kim nor Wilfred would ever have the chance to hold, to kiss on the cheek, or to blow raspberries on his belly. He should have never died so early.

While carrying the weight and burden of Oliver and Aberdeen's losses, tragedy struck again as we suffered yet another loss in late February and it was beyond anything we had ever previously experienced. Our best friends, Adam and Jackie, with whom we have been in house church for the last twelve years, lost their 15-year old son, Abbott, in an unexpectedly tragic accident.

Abbott's death completely and utterly devastated us.

I remember being in the hospital waiting room that night when the trauma team came in and told us that they could not save him. It didn't seem real. It actually seemed incomprehensible. I sat on the uncomfortable arm of a cheaply made, mauve hospital chair and stared lifelessly out of the window and thought, "How do we even do this?" We were entering uncharted territory, where none of us had ever previously traveled. And a year later, here we are, still traveling through this uncharted territory together, in patient, abiding love. But it has been the hardest road we have ever traveled with each other.

The pain and tragedy of death seemed to have us in its grip in that fateful season. And there was even more heartache that had been encircling us through it all.

Jeremy, another great friend who has been in our house church for the last twelve years with his wife, Jess, and their two elementary-aged boys, was arrested in his position as the Chief of Narcotics with the Columbus Police Department.

Jeremy got addicted to legally prescribed painkillers, which then led to him increasingly feeding his addiction by stealing confiscated, illegal narcotics from the evidence room to which he had access in his position. Jeremy was convicted and sentenced to time in jail.

And I honestly wondered how, or even *if*, we could ever make it through the crushing burden of all these catastrophes that were resolved to bury us.

While Jeremy was in jail, and as we cared for Jess and the boys, we walked with Adam and Jackie through the immense pain, suffering, anger, and doubt that we all carried with us. And that is what the spring and summer of 2017 looked like. It was difficult. It was a journey through the valley of the shadow of death and we carried the accumulating heartache of loss and sadness with us every step of the way.

And then August came like Erebus looking for a knockout punch.

What started as a much needed respite, backpacking with Adam and a couple other friends for a week in the heart of the Alaskan backcountry, turned into yet another crushing blow when I returned home and found out that my 43-year old work partner, Jenny, with whom I had worked side-by-side for the last eight years, was told that she had cancer in her lung and liver. The diagnosis came out of nowhere, as she had been in remission from breast cancer for almost five years. But within eight weeks of her initial diagnosis, the cancer moved to her brain and she died just before Thanksgiving.

I know it sounds like a lot.

It has been.

It has been *a lot*.

I have shed more tears this past year than I had collectively in my first 43-years of life. Without question, it was the hardest year of my life.

But I don't want to pretend as if what I experienced is the greatest pain and suffering in human history.

It isn't.

I acknowledge that.

There are so many people, maybe even some of you, who have suffered, or who are currently suffering, in ways unimaginably more than me.

The point is not in trying to determine who has experienced greater pain and suffering in their life. That is futile endeavor that completely misses the point. Rather, it is to add my story among stories, as a humble contribution to our shared human experience of navigating life's painful valleys.

Each of us know what it is like to hurt.

To be wounded.

To be burdened.

To groan.

To cry.

And whether it is the pain of losing a loved one, the agony of feeling trapped and helpless in your life situation, the battle of Stage 4 breast cancer, or the suffocation and anxiety caused by the hostilities and divisions of our country, by our rat race culture, or by the constant stress of trying to make ends meet or to raise kids, we are all in this human experience together.

But it is difficult to not lose heart when everything feels so overwhelming. Our lives can feel so far from what our hearts desire, so far from what our souls crave.

And then, as if that is not enough, right in the middle of all this pain and chaos and division and stress that surround us, we are confronted with the seemingly impossible words of Jesus reminding us that he came to give us *life to the fullest, life in abundance.*

Believe me. I can hear your chorus of groans and your heavy sighs. If you are anything like me, you wonder how in the world you can experience anything close to *life to the fullest* when your tank is running on half-empty, at best, or running on fumes, at worst? How in the world can you experience anything remotely close to *life in abundance* when there is just so much pain, so much suffering, and so much anxiety and stress through it all?

But the words of Jesus kept haunting me and confronting me in a tireless, unending refrain, "*I have come that you might have life and have it abundantly.*"

Okay. Sure. We long and hunger and desire for a *life of abundance*, but it seems like a monumental impossibility. It seems like the naive sentiment of a simple man living two millennia ago who is woefully detached from our postmodern sensibilities.

Even still. I long for that kind of life.

My deepest longing is to be enveloped in the perfect love of God. My greatest hunger is to experience and live in the *completeness, wholeness, and harmony* of the Divine, not just in my own life, but in all of my relationships and with all of creation. My steadfast desire is to, not dismiss or minimize the pain and suffering and anxiety in the world, but to be an ever-present and humble student who learns how to see beauty, and who then learns how to share it through my words and how I live my life, even when the wreckage continues to accumulate around me.

If there is another reality that surrounds us, that holds us, that invites us in to unending life and beauty, that transcends every division and animosity and hostility, that opens us up to new ways of living, how do we even begin to find it, and then how do we begin to live it and invite others into it?

The surprising discovery is that, even in the heartache, even in the hostility, even in the division, and even in the midst of violence and oppression, experiencing *life to the fullest*, a life of *shalom,* is not just possible, it can be our present reality. But in order to discover it, we must learn how to see and live differently, moment by moment, for the transformation of our lives, our families, our relationships, and our communities.

That is the intention of this book.

But first, let me tell you what this book is not.

It is not a self-help book. It is not a five-point sermon with fill-in-the-blanks. It is not a book that is going to tell you what you need to do to "fix" yourself and then the step-by-step guide to "fix" the world around you.

This is a book that will guide you, that will lead you, but will never force you or coerce you into anything. This book may ask more questions than what it answers. It may even cause *you* to ask more questions than you have answers for yourself.

But at the very heart of this book is one underlying question that lingers behind every chapter, "Is it possible to experience *life to the fullest*, a life of *shalom*, in the middle of so much pain and suffering, in the middle of so much hostility and division, and in the middle of so much stress and anxiety?"

And then surrounding that central question are so many more questions.

Is it possible to move beyond labels, hierarchies, stereotypes, antagonisms, and divisions and begin to see people differently and make strides toward a greater unity between us?

Is it possible, in the wreckage around us, to find this *life to the fullest*, this *life of shalom*, when so much of organized religion seems to have guided us poorly, led us astray, and become so irrelevant to our culture?

Is it possible to ever experience *life to the fullest* once you have been through painful and traumatic life situations or suffering? Or, are we destined for lives in which our pain and suffering are an end destination?

Is it possible to ever experience joy again, without leaving our pain and suffering behind us and then constantly forcing a smile, as if everything is great in our lives?

How can prayer center us and help us enter into a constant union and communion with the Divine that begins to birth the *shalom* of God within us?

How can the experience of *shalom* lead to a deeper life of transformation and invite us to become who we were always meant to be?

How can living in *shalom* open our eyes and awaken our hearts to the glory and beauty that surround us each day?

How does a deeply rooted and intimately connected community, or family, nourish and strengthen us to experience greater depths of *shalom*?

How does the experience of *shalom*, not only transform us individually and relationally, but also begin to transform our communities and our world?

I know this may seem like an impossible task. And by the way things appear in the world right now, you may believe this is actually an impossible endeavor. But, it is my hope that through the words on these pages, we will find space to humbly walk together, to find our collective breath, and save our souls.

A few years ago my then four-year old son and I went on our very first overnight backpacking adventure. I can't underscore how important this first trip was for us. I am a serious back-packer. I have been all throughout the United States in some of the most beautiful places on earth, completely cut off from civilization and communication, fighting with grizzlies and running with elk and caribou. Well, I haven't fought grizzlies, nor have I run with elk and caribou, but I have been dangerously close to them!

Anyway, this first overnight backpacking trip with Will was very important to me because I didn't want it to be a bad experience for him on his first time out. Of course we had previously set up the tent and camped in our backyard several times and he really enjoyed that, but leaving the familiarity of our house and going into areas in which he was unfamiliar was a complete wild card.

We drove an hour away from our house and ended up in the Hoosier National Forestry in south-central Indiana. This area is beautifully wooded and hilly and perfect for a first-timer. I could tell Will was excited based on how much he talked during the hour that it took to drive there. He peppered me with one million, four-year old questions that ranged from what we were going to eat to how we were going to brush our teeth. He was so pumped up.

When we pulled into the parking area he was already out of his car seat and standing by the car in wild excitement. He put on his jacket and asked me to help him with his backpack. I helped him and then put on my own backpack. We were off. It was a cool spring evening, not quite sunset, and everything was exploding to life around us. It was absolutely perfect. Will knew it as well.

Every thirty seconds for the next hour, and this is no exaggeration, Will kept yelling out, "For Heaven's sake! This is soooo awesome! For Heaven's sake! This is soooo awesome!"

That may have been one of the greatest moments of my life. Sure, I was glad that Will was off to a great start, but it was so much more than that. In Will, I saw who I longed to be as an adult. Even though we walked through thick mud and miles of thorn bushes that lined the trails, he just keep shouting how awesome his experience was.

Will was unknowingly showing me how far I have traveled from the mystery and wonder of this life. And while I was preoccupied with mud and thorn bushes, Will was preoccupied with wonder in the joyful exuberance of a child.

I am so there with you, brother. Thank you for teaching me to see differently when all I could see in that moment was the mud caked on my boots and the blood running from my arm. You were exactly right, "This is soooo awesome! This is soooo awesome! For Heaven's sake, this is soooo awesome!"

And I really mean it.

I hope you find this book intellectually and spiritually stimulating, as well as emotionally engaging and, at times, even entertaining. And, of course, I pray that, like Will, this journey will guide you into a deeper, richer, and more abundant way of living this life.

I am honored to be journeying with you.

Peace and love,

Brandon
April 2018

CHAPTER 1

Learning to See Beauty in the Wreckage

Never forget: We are alive within mysteries.
WENDELL BERRY

You have never been separate from God except in your mind.
FR. RICHARD ROHR

I remember walking into my backyard one early summer afternoon when I was six-years old. I walked passed the clothesline that held the nearly dry sheets that danced in freedom and swayed in grace with the gently blowing breeze. It was a profound metaphor in that moment of my life. I felt fully and completely alive. With my back to the ground, enveloped by the cool green grass, I stared into the vast, blue sky painted with puffy, white cumulus clouds that seemed to completely surround me. It was in that moment, on that infinitesimally small patch of earth, where I felt wholly embraced in the perfect freedom and perfect love of God.

I have always wondered why that particular memory stayed with me even unto this day. What was it about that simple and seemingly uneventful moment that still has my heart? What was so transformative about that afternoon that it still taps into my soul's deepest longing? And why do I, in my spirit, keep going back to that place behind my late 1970's home where all I did was lie in the grass and stare at the sky?

To be honest, I think about this moment all of the time, even now as an older, more cynical, but hopefully wiser adult.

In retrospect, I know it was so much more than an experience or a feeling in a single, fleeting moment.

The love of God was enveloping me and embracing me. And even though I was only six-years old, I knew it intuitively. I knew it objectively. I knew it deep within my soul. And the reason I knew it was because I had already been exposed to so much darkness just beyond the confines of my backyard.

I was the youngest in a neighborhood full of older kids who had already unceremoniously baptized me into the knowledge of profanity, pornography, sex, drugs, and suicide. They knew words that described things I could have never imagined, but then had the magazines and their own stories to back it up. Even more, one high schooler a few houses down, who was in a wanna-be 80's glam rock band (big hair/black leather), was usually high on drugs, while another high schooler at the end of the road killed himself, which explains why I walked into so much sadness when I went over to his house to play with his younger brother.

I knew darkness at a young age. I knew things I didn't even have the words to describe yet. I discovered sexual perversion and objectification. I experienced the brokenness and heartache of families. I was surrounded by hopelessness and sadness. And I saw the tears. One could cynically say that there is no way a six-year old could ever know so much at such a young age, but I did. If I didn't fully understand the depth of pain and brokenness like an adult does, I could certainly feel the weight of it on my heart.

And that is enough.

That is why I believe that it was in that place, in my backyard, lying in the grass, when I was six-years old, where I knew for the first time, definitively, that heaven and earth overlapped and that God was pouring out and showering me in presence and love, because it contrasted the heavy, dark clouds of pain and sadness that hung over the homes on Indiana Avenue.

The truth is that no matter what else was going on around me or in the world, it was in that place, at that precise moment, where I knew without question in my heart, in my mind, and in my soul that I was wholly embraced in the love of God.

I was in a place where I felt alive.

And it is possible that you have had a moment in your life in which heaven and earth came together as well. It may have been a fleeting moment in which you had a small taste of something eternal that you couldn't quite describe, but that you wished you could experience once again in fullness. It may have been a moment in which you experienced a feeling of wholeness or completeness or harmony in your life or in a relationship. It may have been a moment in which you experienced an inner peace and freedom that seemed to transcend everything that was going on around you, no matter how chaotic or painful. It may have been a moment in which you experienced a grace, a mercy, a forgiveness, a love that you never knew previously existed.

Those moments were the *shalom* of God.

Shalom is the wholeness, completeness, and harmony of our relationship with God which then extends outward in our relationship with people and all of creation.

But never having experienced, or noticed, the *shalom* of God is not a disqualifier, because despite who you are, where you came from, what your background is, or the life situation in which you grew up, this embrace, this freedom, this love has always been present with you and has always surrounded you, whether you have known it, whether you have acknowledged it, or whether you have opened yourself up to it or not.

And the Divine Source of this love has been there all along, completely enveloping us, fully immersing us, and never abandoning us, despite each of us, slowly and progressively, many times unknowingly, never knowing of it, losing sense of it, becoming closed off to it, or turning away from it.

That is the great casualty of this life.

We have become disconnected from the Divine Source of this great embrace. And it is this disconnection that, no matter the paths we have traveled or how it happened in each of our lives, has steadily closed us off from the life we were always meant to live, the life we were always meant to experience, in the *shalom* of God.

Instead of lives immersed in love, overflowing in joy, bathed in peace and contentment, and baptized in grace, it is possible that we have only walked in shallow puddles, while longing for ocean depths.

Instead of abundant lives in which our senses are fully awakened and fully alive, experiencing this beautiful world, this wonderful life in its fullest sense, it is possible that we have become increasingly desensitized to, and uninspired by, the miracle and majesty that we awaken to each morning. And many times, this has caused us to pursue other avenues that artificially stimulate us and close us off to the richness and bounty of this life.

Instead of lives in perfect union with the Divine, that then extend outward through each of us in all of our relationships in peace and wholeness and completeness and harmony in all things, it is possible that our disunion with the Divine has led to disunion in our relationships with people and all of creation.

LIFE CAN FEEL LIKE A STRUGGLE

The truth is that life can feel like a real struggle sometimes. And I am certain I am not shocking you when I say that.

Instead of it feeling like grace, life can many times feel like punishment, judgment, and condemnation. Instead of it feeling like love, life can many times feel like anger, hatred, disappointment, and agony. Instead of it being full of opportunity, life can many times feel like closed doors, empty promises, and dead ends. Instead of it being an invitation into something greater, life can many times feel quite average, extraordinarily ordinary, and like you are just barely making it through the day, barely making ends meet, or barely hanging on.

Instead of us finding life that comes from prayerfully breathing in peace, life can many times feel like anxiety and suffocation. Instead of us finding life in respite and contentment in the space of solitude and silence, life can many times feel like an addiction to stimulation and busyness. Instead of us finding vibrancy and beauty in whole and harmonious relationships and communities, life can many times feel as if the only thing that matters is the individual pursuit.

Even more, we live in increasingly hostile and divided times that feed upon the carnage of our collective anger and unending outrage at people, people-groups, politics and politicians, and countries and world leaders. Our lives, our relationships, and our views of the world have been largely co-opted, and dare I say controlled, by social media, news media, and by those who have interests in stoking our fury.

And we are the casualties, individually, relationally, and communally.

Our lives can feel so far from what our hearts desire, so far from what our souls crave.

We have been, in a very real way, walking through a mine-field with enemy fire passing by us with every step, ripping us away from *shalom*, tearing us from this peace of wholeness and completeness and harmony in all things, this marriage of heaven and earth, this experience of eternal life presently. Sometimes we are hit and wounded, but at other times the ground explodes beneath our feet and it seems as if we have been completely taken down with no way out and no one to help us.

We are those who have been wounded by the words and actions of others. We are those who have been wounded by loved ones who have abandoned us. We are those who have been wounded by the ways others have taken advantage of us. We are those who have been wounded by substance abuse. We are those who have been wounded by our addictions. We are those who have been wounded by our pride and self-sufficiency.

We are those who have been wounded by the expectations others have for us. We are those who have been wounded by a negative self-image or self-doubt, sometimes leading to self-hatred, self-mutilation, and even suicide attempts. We are those suffering from the wounds of broken promises, broken rela-tionships, and failed marriages. We are those suffering from the wounds of physical, emotional, and sexual abuse. We are those who have been literally brought to our knees in grief and heart-ache when our friends and family are diagnosed with a terminal disease or die an unexpected death. We are those who are many times consumed with antipathy, animosity, and maybe even hatred toward those who are different than us, whether that be religiously, politically, racially, or ideologically.

And many times, it's hard to remember, let alone believe, that there is anything better than the hostilities we entered from birth.

Our wounds and pain, our cynicism and skepticism, our apathy and indifference, our anger and resentments have become normal parts of our lives through the years, for some people more than others, of course. But, we are all victims to the great tragedy and its wreckage to one degree or another. And it is easy to become jaded and hardened throughout the years, cynical about the present, and completely resigned to a fractured and divided future. So much so, we can begin to believe that life is something we try to endure, rather than something we still have the opportunity to live to the fullest in the present. And that is the lie we begin to believe, and then the way we begin to see everything around us.

THE DANDELION STORY

I remember one spring when we first moved into the house in which we currently live.

The backyard was a blanket of yellow dandelions.

I hated it.

I freaking hated it.

But first, as a proper backdrop, my dad is a meticulous and obsessive manicurist of fine lawns. And as you can probably imagine, I grew up just like him. I detested this vile weed that was bent on overtaking my dream of a gentle and unbroken sea of green surrounding our house.

This was the case each day as I turned onto the street leading to our new house. It wasn't just the mental frustration of having so many dandelions in my yard. It was, in a very real way, a physical frustration.

I could feel the frustration deep within my bones.

One Saturday morning, and very likely the day I was planning to treat the lawn to kill the weeds, our sweet five-year old Caroline gazed in wonder out the window. I wasn't immediately sure what she was looking at, but then it became obvious, as she said in the most innocent and exuberant voice, "Those are the most beautiful flowers I have ever seen, daddy!"

I sat there in silence.

What a punch to the gut. I was completely and utterly caught off guard.

But Caroline was exactly right. Why did I not see it that way myself? How could I have been looking at something so unimaginably and miraculously beautiful the entire time, but yet been so viscerally disgusted by the sight of it? What I saw as a nuisance weed that needed to be eliminated immediately, Caroline saw as a real life floral tapestry in her own yard that amazed and delighted her.

That may have been the first time in my life when I realized how dramatically our "seeing" alters how we perceive and experience this life.

Unlike me, Caroline had not accumulated the years and years of baggage that influenced and shaped how she viewed the world, how she viewed other people, or how she was experiencing her young life. Caroline was able to see a world surprising her with the blessing of tiny, yellow flowers in her very own yard! She could see beauty clearly, while my distorted lenses saw nothing but a hideous curse that had to be dealt with.

Is it not amazing how two people can look at the same exact thing, yet see it so differently?

Maybe that's why most children have an easier time finding those places where heaven and earth overlap, where they experience perfect freedom and perfect love, where they discover the completeness and wholeness and harmony in all things, because they are not so battle-torn and war-weary. They still have unjaded eyes that are open wide and that can still clearly see the world without the fractured lenses that distort how they see people, situations, and the world around them.

The truth is that children are still open to the possibility of awe and wonder, the inherent goodness in all people and things, and a sense that the only moment that matters is the one they are living in at that exact moment.

It's no wonder Jesus said that unless we all become like little children we will never get to experience this great embrace of heaven and earth. We will never be able to presently enter into the perfect freedom and perfect love of God. We will never be able to receive the *shalom* he has promised us. Becoming like a child opens our hearts and awakens our lives to awe and wonder, allows us to rediscover the inherent goodness in all people and things, and births in us a sense that the only moment that matters is this moment right now.

But is this really even possible?

TOO MUCH HEARTACHE, RIGHT?

It's certainly one thing to be told that each day is grace, full of opportunity, an invitation into something so much greater, and that the *shalom* of the Divine is all around us and holding us and sustaining us, but quite another to actually be able to enter into that kind of life. Sure, the dandelion story is beautiful and a really nice sentiment, but there is simply too much wreckage and too much heartache around us for that kind of unrealistic idealism.

While I admit that I am a wild idealist, and my wife would probably say that I am idealistic to a fault, I will always stand uncompromisingly in the gap between *what is* and *what could be*. I will always look hopefully toward a restored future with the resolve that we can begin living that kind of life right now in the present. However, I do not stand in this place completely oblivious or in blind ignorance of reality.

I see the wreckage around me and I feel the great burden of it every single day. I know you do as well. We live in a world of immense tension and great suffering, a world literally caught between heaven and hell.

And sometimes there are just no words. Our souls just ache.

Today as I write these words I am one degree of separation away from friends whose marriages are wrecking or are completely wrecked, friends who have children growing up without the support or involvement of the other parent and who are suffering through the emotional pain of it, a friend who just overdosed on drugs a few months ago and is now in prison, another friend who was just charged with multiple drug-related felonies, friends and family who are battling for their lives with cancer, our best friends who just lost their teenage son in a fatal accident, my work partner of eight years who just died of cancer leaving a husband and two middle-school children, another friend with three young children who just lost her husband to brain cancer, a friend who just died in a car accident a couple of months ago, a friend who only has weeks left to live because of bone cancer, friends who are unemployed, friends who suffer from mental illness and depression, and friends who have children who have been suicidal in the last few months.

Believe me. I get it. I really get it.

I am not asking you to pretend that there is not horrific pain in the world or to simply ignore the immense suffering in this life. I not only acknowledge it, but I feel it down deep in my soul. There is a literal hell around us that is aggressively trying to break us apart.

ANOTHER LIFE

But surprisingly, astonishingly, maybe even ridiculously, Jesus said that, even in the wreckage of death and destruction, even in the throes of pain and suffering, he came so that we may have lives that are, not just full, but lives that are *overflowing* and *abundant*.

So while we hold together the tension of smiles and tears, the tension of joy and pain, the tension of celebration and mourning, the tension of happiness and sadness, the tension of life and death, we are still, even now, being wholly embraced, completely enveloped, unceasingly pursued, and graciously invited into the perfect love and *shalom* of God through it all.

You may find that incredibly hard to fathom, but listen. Despite the wreckage around us, there is another reality surrounding us, immersing us, in unending life and beauty. It is a reality that longs to revive our broken and wounded hearts so that they may beat again. It is a reality that washes over our blinded eyes so that we may see again. It is a reality that is overflowing and abundant in an ever-present completeness and wholeness and harmony in all things. It is a reality that straightens every path, that stands against and presses into the dark, hostile, and oppressive forces of the world, and extends justice and righteousness for all people.

We live in a world that explodes with great artistry and creativity. It is a world that offers limitless freedom and opportunity. It is a world that flows with the greatest expressions of love and goodness. It is a world with incomparable life and beauty. And we have been invited, to not just see it with new eyes, but to begin living abundantly within it, and then helping others to see it and experience it as well. Yes, even in the wreckage, even in the very worst circumstances, and even through immense and immeasurable pain, we have all been invited to presently enter the great embrace of heaven and earth, together.

And this embrace is no different than the one that so tenderly held me in my lawn that day as a fully awake and fully alive six-year old. It held me and nurtured me then, but began pursuing me through the years, as I grew distant, hard-hearted, angry, prideful, and self-serving. I didn't have the eyes to see it, though. The only thing that changed through the years… was me. The open arms of the father were always outstretched, waiting for me to receive him, and continually longing to hold me again.

THE WINDING PATH

But the path leading back to that place was not a straight line, nor was it pain-free. It never is. We can't snap our fingers or will ourselves into eternal living. It is a daily pursuit that can be completely brutal. It can tear your heart out, rip up your insides, and make you ask questions about who you are, what you are doing, and why you are doing it. I have asked those questions myself. But this winding path requires patience and trust, because we all walk at a different pace, and sometimes we may take a different route than another. So be kind to yourself on this journey. There is no judgment as we walk this road together.

For me, it has been a road of humbling myself, self-reflection and contemplation, crucifixion and resurrection. And all of those words are just ways of saying that I needed to take an honest and humble look at myself to see who I had become, what I was becoming on my own. I desperately needed to discover what was keeping me from living a full and abundant life, keeping me from returning to the embrace of perfect freedom and perfect love, keeping me from receiving the *shalom* of God in the present.

My wife would frequently catch me sitting at the dinner table by myself staring out the window into the backyard many times over the last ten years. I wasn't depressed. I wasn't having a midlife crisis in my 30's. I just had so many questions and I felt like I was completely suffocating.

I found it hard to find happiness and joy.

It seemed as if my life was about enduring each day and I was only happy when anticipating something big or exciting. I battled through each day in hopes of some larger outcome. My happiness and joy were predicated only by what I wanted, or by what I believed I deserved or needed out of life. I was so blind. I could not see the beauty around me. I was so ignorant of the miracle and mystery in which I lived and breathed.

I had become bored and discontented with this life.

But there was this moment when it all started to change for me. I was in the family room after supper with my two daughters. They were playing with each other on the floor, but it was the kind of playing that just grates on the nerves of a parent. And if you are a parent of little kids you know exactly what I mean. There is nice, quiet playing and then there is the loud, blood-curdling, excessive playing. This was the latter.

I was tired from a long day at work and I really didn't feel that well. To be honest, I had been wishing it was a bit later so I could just put them to bed. I am not exactly sure what hit me at that exact moment, but I closed my eyes and rested my head on the back of the couch and just listened. I heard Caroline's sweet voice. I heard Anna laughing at her. I could hear my wife cleaning up in the kitchen. I could hear Aberdeen, my dog, running around and barking at the girls. It was complete chaos, but the most beautiful chaos I had ever heard.

Tears ran down my face and I thanked God.

I was there again. I was in that place. Life was far from perfect, but I was fully present and I was being wholly embraced. There was an abundance in that ordinary moment that was deep and overflowing. It was so good.

I felt like Emily Webb from the Thornton Wilder play *Our Town*. But, rather than looking back in pain and regret, like Emily Webb, for blindly missing the treasure of every moment before it was too late, I was resolved to begin living this life to the fullest while I still had the opportunity and to begin learning how to see and experience it in its fullness, even when it is tough, even when it is painful, even when I hurt, even when I want to give up. My life was going to change. My mind needed to change. I needed a new heart. I needed eyes that could see clearly. I longed for happiness. I longed for joy. I longed for presence. And at that moment, I knew it was possible in my adult life, in ways I had never imagined.

That is where my pursuit began, on the couch in the middle of chaos, in the least likely place to discover joy and gratitude.

What a contrast from the green grass and gentle winds forty years ago when God first had my heart, but this time it was sweeter. I understood it better. I appreciated it so much more.

WHAT ABOUT YOU?

Maybe you once had that experience, as well. Maybe you have had a moment in the middle of your own personal chaos or during a very ordinary moment and knew that life could be so much better, so much richer, so much fuller, so much more abundant than anything you had previously experienced. But, through the constant wreckage of this life, it was lost or forgotten. Maybe it just slowly faded away or died with cynicism or doubt or frustration or with a broken heart. Maybe you just gave up on it because there are too many forces in your life that are trying to break you down and make you unhappy or anxious or stressed or depressed.

But this idea of *life to the fullest* is still the deepest longing of your soul.

What if I told you that this kind of life is still possible? What if I told you that there is a life, a beautiful life, that has been surrounding you since you were born, and it is within your reach just waiting to be received, not in fleeting moments, but in every moment?

What if I told you that, even in the midst of your own pain and suffering, even in your own personal and relational struggles, even through the busyness and rat-race of life, even in the middle of a hateful and hostile and divided world, there is a beautiful reality to be discovered and breathed in at this present moment?

What if I told you that there is a wholeness and completeness and harmony with the Divine, the *shalom* of God, that is all around you just waiting for the receiving that can change how you see and experience this life, how you relate to others, and how you move out in purpose each day?

It is here and it is an ever-present gift to receive, but one which must be discovered. But in order to discover, one must learn how to see differently in this fractured and divided world. But, this pursuit begins in a posture of humble receiving. And that will be our pursuit together, as we navigate through our pain, carry on in our suffering, and journey through the ordinary and the chaos. For there is immense beauty and life and abundance that is immersing us and washing over us, moment by moment, even as we walk through the wreckage.

QUESTIONS

1. Have you ever experienced a moment of perfect freedom and perfect love in your life, as if heaven and earth came together, even if for a split second? If so, describe it? How did you feel in that moment? If you have never had that experience, how does the thought of experiencing wholeness, completeness, and harmony in your life and relationships sound to you?

2. As you think about your life, in what ways do you feel like you have experienced less than a life of wholeness, completeness, and harmony?

3. On a daily basis, how does news and social media make you feel? In what ways are they counterproductive to *shalom* (wholeness, completeness, and

harmony in all things)- individually, relationally, and communally?

4. What wreckage have you experienced in your life and how does it still affect and influence you?

5. Based upon the words in this chapter, what are your expectations with the rest of the book? What gives you the greatest hope?

CHAPTER 2

The Unity of All Things

A person can become accustomed to the worst of lives just as long as everyone around him lives the same way.

TOLSTOY

In Christ's family there can be no division into Jew and non-Jew, slave and free, male and female. Among us you are all equal. That is, we are all in a common relationship with Jesus Christ.

PAUL THE APOSTLE

Every time I go backpacking, I find myself in the some of the most remote and isolated backcountry in the world.

On my most recent endeavor to Wrangell-St. Elias National Park and Preserve in southeast Alaska, I was more distant and separated from civilization than I had ever been in my entire life. The closest town, McCarthy, Alaska (population 45) was 50 miles from where we would be backpacking over the week and was only reachable by bush plane.

I don't know if you have ever had any type of similar experience, of finding yourself literally cut off from the world, from communication, from news media, from geopolitical rumblings, from domestic unrest, from political upheaval. But it is both a liberating and terrifying experience.

In one sense, there is a sweet relief in finding solace in the stillness of the wilderness. Yet, in another sense, there is a profound unease upon re-entering the "real world."

It is as if this retreat into the wild always provides a necessary cleansing or washing from the accumulated daily muck and mire and mudslinging of our culture, but then is unceremoniously followed by the ugly realization that the mudslinging continues all the while. There is a sad inevitability of having to walk back into it.

And I was told as much upon my first communication back into civilization when one of my friends texted me the following words, "After the political events of this past week, I suggest heading straight back into the wilderness."

I seriously thought about it after taking a quick look at the news and social media.

There is a crushing agony to experiencing so much stillness and peace and serenity, of being fully enveloped and immersed in the miracle and mystery of life, but then walking back into so much anger, hatred, and division.

THE TENSION OF TWO REALITIES

There are two very different, very distinct, parallel realities that exist in tension.

But too many times, it seems as if the only reality we see on a daily basis, the only reality we have been made to believe truly exists, the only reality we are told that we can live and participate, is this embattled reality that is ravaging us and swallowing us whole. And to be honest, when we trust the news, social media, and our hyper-rationalistic culture, this seemingly all-powerful, destructive reality, which is tearing us apart at the seams and ripping us away from the present experience of *shalom*, becomes our only reality.

We are continually bombarded with notions that spirituality is naive and narrow-minded and passe' to the modern intellectual mind. The wisdom of ancient mystics, who taught that union and communion with the Divine is our soul's greatest longing, has been passed off as ancient ideas. Ideals, such as love and peace, that transcend every categorization, every division, and every conflict, have been dismissed as unrealistic, Pollyanna pursuits in dealing with our "real world issues."

But what do you do when the deepest longings of your soul, of being wholly enveloped in perfect freedom and perfect love, of experiencing the sweet embrace of heaven and earth, of awakening to the richness and abundance of this life, seem like a gigantic impossibility?

What do you do when your deepest, most essential hunger is *shalom*, not just in your own life, but in your relationships, in your community, and in the world, but all you see is the accumulating wreckage that surrounds you day after day?

What do you do when you have tasted something in the past that is so sweet and so desirable that it resurrected within you a profoundly eternal sense of goodness and awe and wonder and light, but the dark clouds of division and hostility are dimming that light?

If there is another reality that surrounds us, that holds us, that invites us to unending life and beauty, that is our soul's deepest longing, that transcends every division and animosity and hostility, why does it appear as if it has been eclipsed by the darkness of antipathy, hatred, rage, and disunion? If there is another reality, why have so many given up on it? If there is another reality, why does this darkness appear to be our *only* reality?

LABELS AND DIVISIONS

I remember sitting in an undergraduate philosophy class at Hanover College in which the professor, discussing the limitations, nuances, and intricacies of human language, explained to us that while we English speakers have only one word for the frozen precipitation that falls from the sky, snow, the Inuit people have over 50 words to describe every variation and type of snow.

I have to admit at being amazed at such detail of observation and subtlety of experience.

There is something fascinating about being able to use descriptive words and language to paint a mental picture for others that is rich and vibrant in its specificity and detail. As a writer, I am continually reminded of the importance of words and how appreciative readers are at being able to participate in an experience, at being able to make a visceral connection to a story, and at being able to imagine the intricate details of an image.

All through words.

Words can bring observations and experiences to life.

However, our diversity in words and language also make us expert classifiers and near-obsessive labelers.

And you may be wondering why you picked up on a bit of cynicism with that last sentence.

While we may not all have the exhaustingly expressive, yet delightfully observant-of-every-fine-detail chops of Dostoevsky, we all have an almost innate need for describing things. We are hardwired, it seems, with the ability to observe, discriminate, label, and classify. And of course this is not inherently bad but actually serves many good and useful purposes.

However, our specificity in precise and meticulous observations, our keen eye at discriminating, our acuteness in classifying and labeling can actually, consequently and unintentionally, limit our experiences and create divisions of reality.

Rather than seeing people as they are, rather than enjoying experiences for what they are, we very naturally, maybe even unconsciously, begin to divide all things into categories and groups. And when we do this, it can very easily lead to the creation of dualities (this one is good and that one is bad) and hierarchies (this one has more value than that one). It can also ultimately lead to antagonisms and conflicts among theses divisions. And this can happen simply by the categories in which we place ourselves and other people and then by what we subsequently believe about them, or are told to believe about them, based solely upon how they are described, labeled, or categorized.

THE CONSERVATIVE, REPUBLICAN EVANGELICAL

The reason I know this to be true, besides seeing it all around me everyday, is that I have experienced the judgment of another person, based solely upon the label I was given.

About twenty years ago a friend and I believed that we should start an organization called *Taking Back America*. We thought that the very best thing for America was for Christians to mobilize politically and make a stronger united effort to influence our governments, schools, and other institutions "for the cause of

Christ." We were very excited about pursuing this endeavor and were planning to have a huge kick-off event with some nationally recognized political speakers, who were Christians, and some critically acclaimed Christian musical acts.

With the planning underway and a few speakers already committed, I contacted a particular artist management company to line up a specific musician that we really loved. I spoke to several different people at this company, telling them all about what we were doing and why we were doing it. I sent them our information and they told me that they would get back with me within a couple of weeks.

But they never did.

Frustrated, as this was the last piece of the puzzle that we needed to begin promoting the event, I called the agency back in order to find out what was taking so long. The lady with whom I had been speaking over the previous weeks finally passed my call over to the agency director. The subsequent conversation left me frustrated and confused.

The director started by saying that he did not believe the musician we were trying to book necessarily agrees with what we were doing or how we were doing it. Perplexed, I asked him to be more specific. He said that neither he, nor the musician, believed that it was a good thing for Christianity to advance politically, adding that they did not think America necessarily had to be "taken back for Christ," by the means we were suggesting.

I continued to press him because I could not understand what he was saying. It was not computing. It would not register. I could not imagine that there could be a different perspective that did not believe Christians ought not take America back and "restore it to the Christian values and ideals we once had." Even more frustrated, I asked him how, exactly, we ought to move forward as Christians in America if we do not do it politically.

He told me something I will never forget. He said, "The kingdom of God is not dependent upon our politics or our governments to move forward." But what followed that sentence was the most despicable form of judgment and lack of grace I have ever experienced.

In response to my serious lack of understanding to his perspective and my continued questioning for clarity, he said, "People like you will never get it."

And that crushed me.

The way we label and classify and categorize people can reinforce, maybe even harden and solidify, what we think about them and what is already in our hearts. They become projections of how we see, experience, and relate to the world, as a divided, fragmented reality.

I was categorized as a Conservative, Republican Evangelical. And because of that label, I was not worth the effort or time because I would "never get it."

Well, I did eventually get it. And rather than continuing the endless cycle of labeling others and diminishing people and causing more anger and division, I want to use that experience to chart a better way forward together.

WE DON'T SEE PEOPLE

We live in a time in which we are hyper-obsessed with how we describe ourselves, how we label others and put them into categories, how we begin to assign worth and value based upon the label a person or group wears and the category in which a person or group identifies.

Even more, we then begin to live in division and conflict, either mentally or physically, with a labeled and categorized person or group, without ever knowing the person behind the label.

The sad and tragic reality is that underneath a label or a classification is a person, a flesh and blood human being, a living and breathing creation with a soul, who has been reduced to a cheap descriptor, who is only seen as an easy label for how they are described, who is stereotyped and caricatured, not for the depth of who they are, or as one uniquely created in the image of God, but as an object that can be disrespected, diminished, and discarded.

God help us.

We are in a very precarious time in history. The discriminating generalizations and xenophobic stereotypes, the widening fissures and the deepening crevasses in relationships, and then the tectonic plates of verbal and physical conflict between people and groups are shaking the foundations on which we stand. We are on the precipice of a cultural civil war and it is a dark manifestation of our fearful individualism, our isolated homogeny, and our dehumanization and devaluation of "those people" (whoever "those people" are, but it seems like there are more "those people" than ever today).

Political ideology is pit against political ideology. Ethnic group is set against ethnic group. The One Percent is put into conflict with the Ninety-nine Percent. All Lives Matter is set against Black Lives Matter and vice versa. Anti-gun supporters are against Pro-gun supporters. Republicans are against Democrats. Democrats are against Republicans. One lifestyle rages against another lifestyle. Religious groups are against atheist groups, and atheist groups are against religious groups.

And the tragedy is that we begin to exist for who we are against.
Against illegal immigrants.

Against homosexuals.

Against liberals.

Against conservatives.

Against evangelicals.

Against Muslims.

Against science.

Against presidents.

Against.

Against.

Against.

And the antagonism never ends.

We are in increasingly cynical, polarized, and confrontational times. Times that have lost innocence and imagination. We, too many times, operate collectively at the lowest common denominator with a survival-of-the-fittest mentality. We do not just oppose others; we diminish their humanity, as if they have no worth or value at all. Our causes, affiliations, and ideologies have become more important and more valuable than human beings themselves. People have become obstacles, and then the necessary casualties, to achieve our agendas, to prove our "rightness" and their "wrongness."

We don't see people as human beings. We only see them for how they are labeled, for the issues they represent, and we believe they must be crushed and defeated.

We have become too deeply entrenched in our individual hatreds. We have sold our souls to the political machines of rancor and antagonism. We have pledged allegiance to our own interests in the world. We spend way too much time on social media fighting and arguing about opinions that really don't matter that much and that actually fracture and divide us further. We have become shackled to religions of rightness, and everyone's wrongness, for too long.

But all the while, these fires rage on day after day and are intentionally doused with the verbal gasoline of minute-by-minute news coverage, the political talking heads, social media algorithms that reinforce our little echo chambers, and the vested interest of every special interest group.

The truth is that *each of these* can be biased in order to further manipulate our feelings and beliefs in how we see others and how we see the world. And they push us to the poles of division and antagonism against one another.

It is a sad reality how weak we are becoming, how eagerly we consume what we are being fed, how easily we allow our moral structures to fall for lack of any substantial foundation, and how quickly we fall victim to the biased narratives.

And the evidences of this fractured and divided reality, which has led to the dehumanization of others and the great divisions between us, are scattered all around us. Every moment of the day, from our social media posts and comments to the ever-increasing brazenness and hostility of our words in real life, there is so much anger and vitriol and animosity and hatred and division that has engulfed us.

It is swallowing us whole.

ERASING DIVIDING LINES

If this rising tide of antagonism is to ever begin receding, if the war around us is to ever cease, if the dividing lines are to ever be erased, if the wreckage is to ever be repaired and restored, it begins with each one of us. here. now.

And if the sweet embrace of heaven and earth is to ever extend wider, if perfect freedom and perfect love is to ever be a shared experience, if *shalom* is to ever go forth into our relationships, into our communities, and into the larger world, and if beauty is to ever be discovered in the wreckage that surrounds us, it has to begin with each one of us.

I am not sure if you have ever considered this, but up until the time of Jesus the trajectory of the biblical narrative was a devolution into division, classification, and labeling that then further disintegrated into either/or thinking, hateful discrimination, fearful xenophobia, we/they mentalities, cyclical conflicts, ethnic and religious prejudices, political animosities, and perpetual wars.

And this cycle played out over and over and over and over.

Does it sound familiar?

But with Jesus, this tired and predictable trajectory ended.

And when I talk about Jesus, I am not referring to anything or anyone but Jesus Christ alone, because so many people, churches, and institutions have twisted Jesus into something he never was. Jesus has been made to promote nationalism, patriotism, socialism, communism, and every kind of violence and war and atrocity on earth. I am not talking about the Jesus that has been misconstrued, caricatured, and misrepresented by any number of churches, denominations, institutional religions, or any other deviation of religion or politics that has abandoned, maligned, or distorted the way of Jesus.

I am talking about the self-sacrificing, other-centered, enemy-loving Christ that existed in perfect *shalom* with the Divine and with all of creation.

Because when we start with that Jesus, we find the most revolutionary, counter-cultural, and radical movement in history.

At the height of hateful discrimination, fearful xenophobia, we/they mentalities, cyclical conflicts, ethnic and religious prejudices, political animosities, and perpetual wars, Jesus started a movement away from classifications, labels, and divisions which then began to erase dividing lines and hierarchies and conflicts, all with the most unlikely people from every different part of life.

Jesus faced, head on, ethnocentrism and racism. Jesus stood up to inequality and social stratification. Jesus embraced the uncivilized, the disabled, the outcast, the stigmatized, the unclean, the infected, the sinner. Jesus even hung out with people who had different ideas than him and who may have even been considered enemies by others. Jesus broke every social norm of every institution and construct of his time.

No longer were people to be labeled or classified, no longer were people to be divided against or placed in hierarchies, no longer were people to live in conflict or hostility, because in the Christ there was a new way of seeing all things that was being brought to life.

In the Christ was the beginning of one new humanity.

No longer were people to be seen as Jew or Gentile, because in the Christ there is one new humanity. No longer were people to be seen as rich or poor, because in the Christ there is one new humanity. No longer were people to be seen as male or female, because in the Christ there is one new humanity. No longer were people to be seen as barbarians or civilized, because in the Christ there is one new humanity. No longer were people to be seen as clean or unclean, because in the Christ there is one new humanity.[1]

ONE NEW HUMANITY

And when one begins to see differently, Christ is all, and is in all. When one begins to see differently, we no longer regard anyone from a worldly point of view. When one begins to see differently, the old ways have gone and the new ways have come. When one begins to see differently, we are able to unite as one and find communion in the life-giving, life-sustaining Christ and in a love and peace that transcends every dividing line. For it is only in that which is transcendent that we can collectively move beyond every division.

That is the radical beauty of the message Jesus preached, that we would no longer be viewed by what label we wear or classification we have been given. We would unite and align in a love that transcends every label, every classification, every ideology, and every division and that guides us in how to see all things differently.

No longer do we see Protestant or Catholic, because in the Christ there is one new humanity.

No longer do we see fundamentalists or liberals, because in the Christ there is one new humanity.

No longer do we see those on the inside or those on the outside, because in the Christ there is one new humanity.

No longer do we see conservative or progressive, because in the Christ there is one new humanity.

No longer do we see legal citizen or illegal alien, because in the Christ there is one new humanity.

No longer do we see Black Lives Matter or All Lives Matter, because in the Christ there is one new humanity.

No longer do we see privileged or underprivileged, because in the Christ there is one new humanity.

No longer do we see gay or straight, because in the Christ there is one new humanity.

No longer do we see transgender or cisgender, because in the Christ there is one new humanity.

No longer do we see religious or atheist, because in the Christ there is one new humanity.

No longer do we see American or Pakistani or Afghani or North Korean or Venezuelan or Russian, because in the Christ there is one new humanity.

For it is through this life-giving, life-sustaining Christ in which all things were created. And by this Christ that all things hold together. And through this Christ that God is restoring all things to himself into a perfect oneness, a perfect wholeness, a perfect unity with no division, no dividing lines, no classifications, and no labels, for those who presently receive this invitation of union, this invitation of *shalom* with the Divine.

Do you see it? *That is the good news.*

And it is precisely in this *good news* where you will find my deep and abiding passion and energy, and where you will discover the uncompromisingly expectant heart of this book, because it is where my joy abounds.

And it is for that reason alone why I will never submit to a defeated, antagonistic, divided reality. It is for that reason why I will not run back into the backcountry of Alaska to escape the hostilities. Because I believe that there is another reality into which we are all invited, and into which we can all presently enter, that resides in love, that moves outward in peace, and that sees and presently experiences this life and all people in oneness.

This is where it all begins.

It is a reality birthed in our union and communion with the Divine and it is for every single individual, for every single relationship, and for every single community, across every culture, every ethnic group, every race, every orientation and lifestyle, and from every tongue, tribe, and nation.

THE WEDDING

There is an ancient story about a time when Jesus, his mother, and a few of his disciples went to a countryside wedding in Cana of Galilee. In the middle of this huge wedding celebration, there was a monumental problem.[2]

They ran out of wine.

Not even one single drop of wine remained.

They completely ran out.

And if there is one thing you do not do at an ancient, near-Eastern wedding, you absolutely, positively do not run out of wine. Such an oversight would bring shame to the family, as well as the bride and groom.

But there is something curious and unbelievably beautiful that happens right in the middle of the impending catastrophe.

Mary, the mother of Jesus, comes to Jesus and urgently shares that they are all out of wine, but Jesus calmly replies, "What does this have to do with me? My time has not yet come?"

Mary then turns to the servants and says, "Do whatever he tells you."

Somehow you just know from Mary's words that everything will be alright. No one will be experiencing any shame or dishonor in the middle of this massive wedding celebration. Jesus will make this thing right. Just do what he says.

Jesus then looks over at six empty twenty-gallon stone jars that are typically filled with water for purification rituals and tells the servants to fill each of them to the very top with water. And they trusted that he knew what he was doing, so they did it.

And you know the rest of the story.

Jesus miraculously turns a whole lot of water into a whole lot of wine (like 120 gallons of the absolute best heavenly wine)!

But there is so much more going on here than what meets the eye.

At the very beginning of the account, the author tells us that this event, which he refers to as the first of Jesus' signs, occurs on the *third day*. And the *third day* to which he is referring is Christ's resurrection, the beginning of new creation, the beginning of this *marriage* of heaven and earth.

Do you see where this is going?

Third day. Resurrection. Big Marriage Party.

In light of the resurrection, this big marriage party, of heaven and earth coming together as one, has already started.

The writer is referring specifically to this marriage of heaven and earth, this sweet embrace of heaven and earth, this union and communion with the Divine into which we all have been presently invited. The celebration of this wedding is all around us right now. The festivities have already begun. And there is singing and drinking and jubilation.

But even while we presently celebrate, even amidst the feasting, the happiness, the joy, and the beauty of this marriage of heaven and earth, there is a tension that threatens to bring down the party in shame and dishonor, there is an impending tragedy that could upend the entire celebration.

Will this tension break apart this marriage?

Will this tension ruin this celebration?

Will this tension stop our dancing and our singing?

Will this tension bring shame and dishonor and tears and regret and pain and suffering?

What do you see?

Are you standing at the empty stone jars and only seeing the impossibility of the situation? Are you standing at the empty stone jars and thinking about the shame and dishonor and regret and pain and suffering that will ruin the marriage and halt the celebration? Are you standing at the empty stone jars next to others who are convinced that the party is over and who are already pointing fingers at who is to blame- the man who drank too much, the woman who took two glasses rather than one glass every time she got a refill, those who just showed up but who weren't invited and drank too much, the person who bought the wine but didn't buy enough?

At the empty stone jars all seems lost. All seems bleak. All seems dire. There may be some anxiety and stress. There may be some worry and fear. There may even be some internal pain and suffering.

What do you see?

Is there a light to be found in all of this darkness? Is there any reason to have hope? Everyone who sees the impossibility of the situation is angry and is beginning to blame others. And as we stand there, we may easily forget that there is a marriage and a celebration that hasn't stopped, that there are even more people dancing and laughing and hugging, that the music is getting even louder, and that the wine is about to get a whole lot better!

What do you see?

There is an entirely new and beautiful and hopeful reality that surrounds us, that envelops us, that will never be consumed or destroyed or defeated in hopelessness. It is alive and it is full and it is abundant. It is a miraculous and mysterious reality that satisfies our deepest longings, that satiates our deepest hunger, that erases every dividing line, that transcends our every difference, and that awakens our souls to the awe and wonder and oneness of all things. And it is the marriage of heaven and earth and the celebration continues all around us.

Can you see it?

QUESTIONS

1. Have you ever experienced the profound tension of peace and contentment, while also experiencing the anger, frustration, and hostility of the world around you? How did each make you feel? How did each affect your views of others or how you view the world?

2. In general, which reality has influenced you the most? And why do you think that is the case?

3. Think of a time when you were on the receiving end of stereotyping, labeling, discrimination, or judgment. How did it make you feel? What did it lead you to think about the other person or a people group?

4. As you think about how you currently see the world, are there individuals or groups against whom you have been antagonistic, hostile, angry, or divided? Even more, are there individuals or groups toward whom you have been hard-hearted, uncharitable, judgmental, or less than loving? What do you believe is the root of your feelings toward these individuals and people groups?

5. How does the understanding of the unity of all things in the Christ begin to challenge or change any of the negative beliefs or attitudes you have held towards individuals or people groups? How does this understanding begin to heal divisions and restore people and people groups?

CHAPTER 3

You Have Been Invited

*You'll never recognize God if you believe
everything people tell you about God.*

TOLSTOY

No one can teach you how to see.

AVATAR

I want to share a couple of stories with you that I recently heard.

A preacher was recounting a time several years ago when, during the "invitation hymn" after the sermon, a lady came forward to be baptized. The preacher had previously heard about this lady, as he had been told that she was currently living with her boyfriend, who was already a member of the church. As they stood together in front of the congregation, the pastor reflected that he knew he "needed to confront her about her sinful relationship."

And that is exactly what he did.

As they exited to change clothes and prepare for the baptism, the preacher cornered her and said, "There is no way I can baptize you unless you quit living in sin."

The couple gave him their assurances that they wouldn't live together. The lady was baptized. And they never went back to his church again.

As if it couldn't get any worse, in the same sermon, the preacher proudly recalled a funeral he was to give to a 19-year old young man he did not know personally, but whom he soon found out was a motorcycle biker.

As the preacher was on his way to the funeral, he detailed his approach to the funeral home. He said that he saw a parking lot full of "stereotypical [bikers] with long hair and tattoos all over the place, right there in public smoking their joints and drinking [beer], with several of them having their girls along with them dressed immodestly on the back of their bikes."

As I listened to these heartbreaking words and the tone in which they were spoken, all I could think was, "Would Jesus ride passed these bikers and their 'immodestly dressed girls' in judgment based upon how they looked and then think that he needed to preach the gospel to them when they come into the funeral home?

Or, would he have gone out to them, embraced them, cried with them, listened to their stories of how they knew the young man, and then told them about the beautiful invitation and present reality of God's kingdom that surrounds them and invites them in?"

To me, the answer is so clear and so evident.

Throughout the Gospels, Jesus was always at the table of invitation with all types of people, but especially those who were regarded as outcasts and those who were stigmatized by society- tax collectors, prostitutes, the unclean, the disabled, and every type of special sin group at that time.

WHO ARE OUR GUIDES?

I wish I could tell you that stories like those above are anomalies. But they are not.

I remember a time, as a young man, when I overheard chatter among people in my church about a lady who was wearing a mini-skirt and how she needed to be told to dress modestly in the "House of the Lord."

As soon as the service ended, an elder of the church approached the young woman, who had never been to our church before, and told her that if she was going to come back she needed to dress appropriately.

She never came back.

I share these stories for a specific reason.

The world in which we live is full of men and women from all walks of life who long for something more than what they awake to each morning. They are people we meet and cross paths with, who have their own struggles, and who know intuitively, who know down deep in their souls, that there has to be so much more to this life.

And they are just like us. People who may have had a moment in their past when heaven and earth overlapped, when they tasted something wonderful and divine, and have been desperately searching to find it again. Even if they couldn't name the experience, or really even describe it, they knew that they wanted to find it again.

But in the very place where they believed they might discover it, the church, they were instead met with judgment, expectations that they must already be perfect, and rules of perfection which they must follow.

And this is one of many reasons why so many have given up on going to church. We are hungry for so much more than what we are finding within their walls.

We are those desperately trying to make sense of this chaotic and upside-down world that feels like it is blowing up all around us. We are those attempting to make sense of faith and spirituality in a world where it looks like there is just too much suffering and too much evil prevailing. We are those searching after something of substance that we hope will lead us into more abundant lives. We are those starving and hungry for *life to the fullest*, those longing to be fully awake and fully alive, and those who want to find a greater sense of wholeness, completeness, and harmony in all things.

But who is guiding us? Who is helping us learn how to see, and then to be, differently in the world?

Religion has largely been more preoccupied with belonging systems and controlling *who's in* and *who's out* and sin management than guiding people through the wreckage, and into a more beautiful, more abundant way of living.

And it is for this reason why I am convinced that, in addition to the masses of people leaving the institutionalized church, the vast majority of visionaries and prophets are outside the walls of the church right now as well.

They are going directly to the people who are deconstructing their faith and who are still searching for something of meaning and substance, and then guiding them into the ways of *shalom*. These visionaries and prophets desperately long for churches to awaken and lead their people and their cities and towns in the ways of *shalom*, and to be instrumental in helping put the broken pieces of their communities back together. And some churches are starting to do just that. But the vast majority are presently too consumed with themselves and their own interests. And to that end, we can no longer wait on churches to figure this out.

A NEW WAY OF SPEAKING

The words of Jesus to the religious capture this tension so perfectly when he says, "You shut the door of the kingdom of [God] in people's faces. You yourselves do not enter, nor will you let those enter who are trying."[1]

Don't get lost here in the language of the kingdom of God. Jesus was speaking to people who understood kings and kingdoms and lords and it all made perfect sense to them at that time.

But that is not the way we speak any more.

The kingdom of God can be understood by us as this present embrace of perfect freedom and perfect love. It is an unconditional and forgiving love that has always been present with us and has always surrounded us, enveloped us, fully immersed us, and never abandoned us. It is the present union and communion with God that transforms us, and then begins to extend outward in wholeness and completeness and harmony in all things. It is the present marriage, the present coming together, of heaven and earth in our lives.

The kingdom of God is shalom. It is the life we were always meant to live, because that is the only place where life to the fullest is found.

So with this phrase, the kingdom of God, Jesus is simply talking about a present life experience that people are searching to discover and trying to enter, but that religion blocks them from ever discovering. And surprisingly, as Jesus says, the religious haven't entered into it either. So not only have the religious not entered into this life of *shalom*, they actually keep others from discovering and entering into it.

The religious may have the very best of intentions, but this embrace, this freedom, this love does not originate *from* them, nor is it entered *through* them. It doesn't come from following the "right rules," or being on the "right religious team," or by avoiding certain "sins."

There is a parable of the kingdom of God that Jesus shares of a man who finds a treasure that had been hidden in a field. Through his own searching, he discovers the riches and then sells everything he has to buy the field in order to have all of the riches of this treasure.[2]

This short story reveals an amazing paradox and a poignant truth about our fundamental humanity and what it means to be alive. *The riches of an abundant life only come through our own searching and willingness to give up everything in order to receive what we have discovered. It doesn't come from anyone else. It can only be discovered by you.*

And that is a game changer.

It is a truth so profound and relevant today because there are many people, even within the churches, who are searching desperately for the wholeness and completeness of a better life, but who do not realize that there is actually something beyond themselves that can satisfy their every longing, that can satiate their deepest hunger, that can awaken their senses to the profound beauty around them. The sad reality, for many, is that this treasure remains hidden because they have been looking in all the wrong places and looking to all the wrong people.

Shalom is not found in a classroom, earned by religious affiliation or practice, received through the proper steps, or handed down from one person to another. It can only be found by the humble, earnest seeker who simply receives that which has been surrounding them the entire time, the *shalom* of God.

In the book *The Practice of the Presence of God*, which is a collection of writings from a 17th century monk named Brother Lawrence, he is quoted as saying, "There is no sweeter manner of living in the world than continuous communion with God. Only those who have experienced it can understand."[3]

Jesus echoes that exact sentiment when he says, "Wide is the gate and broad is the road that leads to destruction, and many enter through it. But small is the gate and narrow the road that leads to life, and only a few find it."[4]

While many wrongly ascribe those words of Jesus to a future heaven and future hell, that is not at all what he is talking about.

Jesus is talking about the difficulty of discovering the present experience of the kingdom of God. Those who have never searched for the life-giving present reality of the kingdom of God, the present life of *shalom*, will continue with lives that move toward, and further compound, destruction and wreckage. But those who continue searching will discover the narrow way, which few actually find, that leads to a sweeter manner of living in constant communion with God. Narrow is that path that leads to life and only those who seek after it will find it.

TAKING BACK BORN AGAIN

There is an absolutely fascinating encounter between Jesus and a high-ranking religious man named Nicodemus. When the religious man approaches Jesus under the cover of night, Jesus says to him, "No one can see, or experience, the *kingdom of God* unless they are born again."[5]

Please, suspend your judgment for a moment, because the phrase *born again* has been tragically hijacked by a political segment of Christianity that has given it a negative and hyper-charged meaning that was never intended. *Born again*, in the proper context, means something so much more beautiful and different than you could ever imagine.

Jesus is saying that we will never be able to *see* or *experience* this *shalom*, that we will never be able to be whole, complete, or in perfect harmony with all things in the present, unless we are born from above, unless we open ourselves in a posture of humility to actually receive this embrace of God in the Spirit.

Even more, Jesus is saying all of this to *a religious man*!

Jesus is saying that it is possible to miss the most important thing underneath the title, the position, the costume, the appearance, the weekly attendance, the revivals, the Sunday School classes, the strategic planning meetings, the offerings, and the smiles and handshakes. And to the extent we have believed any of that extraneous stuff matters to God, we have been mistaken.

It is entirely possible to miss *shalom*, because no matter who you are, you will never discover what you are not actively seeking, even if you believe you are going through all the right steps. Because when religion becomes a pursuit of anything other than seeking to discover the *shalom* of God, it has completely missed the heart of God.

God's intention has only and always been intimate union. It has been for God's presence to be born within each of us. And this intimate, relational union with the Divine is the only place where *shalom* can be found. It is the only place where one can become whole, complete, and in harmony with all things.

It is also the place where each of us are on equal footing before God. It is the place where no one person is any better or worse than another. So no matter how important, how decorated, how influential, how knowledgeable, how righteous, or how powerful any single person may think they are, even if they are preachers or those in leaderships positions, *we are all in the same position together.*

And this understanding begins to help us think differently about *sin* and *forgiveness.*

But again, we are dealing with two negatively hyper-charged and powerfully loaded words that have been force fed into our collective psyche, so allow some space before jumping to any conclusions about what these words actually mean.

RETHINKING SIN

Interestingly, close to eighty-percent of the time the word *sin* is used in the New Testament, it is used as a noun.

This is interesting because we typically hear people talk about *sin* as a verb.

They describe all of the bad things we do that make God angry at us. And inevitably, when people focus on *sin* primarily as a verb, they get obsessed with saying *this sin* is worse than *that sin. This sin* can be overlooked but *that sin* can't. And *this sin* is unforgivable but *that sin* is okay (since we are all doing it).

The original Greek word for *sin*, as a noun, is *hamartia.* It means *to be without a share in*, or *a position where one has missed the mark or strayed.*[6]

Sin is simply a position in which we find ourselves.

It is a position out of alignment with God, or in *disunion* with God. And in that place of disunion, we are the opposite of *shalom*, the opposite of wholeness, completeness, and harmony in all things.

And this begins to open our eyes to the central issue.

It's not that we are horrible wretches for committing all of these terrible sins every day. It is that we are collectively, and equally, in a position of *disunion* with the Divine. And when we live out of this broken relationship, it very naturally begins to look unwhole, incomplete, and inharmonious. It is the natural consequence of us living outside of *shalom.*

That is why God's intention has always been to get rid of *sin,* or to remove the relational barrier between us, because we were always meant to be in *union* with God, where *life to the fullest* is found.

The wisdom of Paul ought to be an eye-opener for each one of us today, because he echoes this exact point when he says that we all fall short of God's glory.[7] We are all in the same position of disunion, equally. There is not one single person who has a position that is any better or any worse than another. And in this position, we are not presently sharing in this *shalom.*

That is sin, as a noun.

So when religious people begin creating these crazy hierarchies of *sin* and telling us that certain people or groups are worse than others, telling us *who's in* and *who's out*, all it does is alienate and devalue people who should not be alienated or devalued. It sends a message that the religious are good and righteous and all the rest of us are sinners who are bad and unworthy. And all that does is create more judgment and condemnation and anger and hostility toward people, which leads to more walls of division between us all.

The point is that when the religious view *sin* primarily, or exclusively, as a verb, they fall back into that old way of labeling, categorizing, ranking, and then dividing. And it completely misses the big picture that we are all in the same position and that the heart of God has always been an invitation back into relational union with every single one of us equally.

Every. Single. One. Of. Us. Equally.

So when we begin to see *sin* correctly, as a place of disunion, we understand there can be no hierarchy of sin or worthiness. We are all disconnected from the Source of Life, and we are in that place together.

Hard stop.

And once we begin to understand this simple truth, it is the place where humility and grace comes to life and shines. It is the place of remarkable beauty and breakthrough. It is the place where all the broken pieces of the world come back together as one, where we learn how to see beauty in the wreckage, and where everyone is welcome to the table of invitation together, without judgment or exclusion, whether you are living with someone, a biker who drinks beer and smokes a little weed, or a young lady wearing a short skirt.

I AM SO SORRY

If this truth has been withheld from you, or if you have received something very different than this message of radical invitation and inclusion, please let me tell you that the grace and love of God has always been with you, has always been for you, and has always surrounded you. The grace and love of God has always been with you, even in your disunion, even when you have felt unworthy, and has always been inviting you back with open arms, as you are, into loving union with the Source of Life.

But there may be some of you, maybe a lot of you, who are reading these words and still carrying around so much pain and so many wounds from past church experiences or past dealings with religious people.

I am deeply sorry and I completely understand.

But.

No matter what you may have been told.

No matter how badly you may have been treated or wounded.

No matter the judgments and accusations that may have been thrown at you.

No matter if you may have been told that you are unworthy or unredeemable.

No matter if you may have been told that God will never forgive you.

Let me tell you emphatically, once and for all, that you are loved and you are already forgiven, as you are.

Every single one of you.

Forgiven.

Past tense.

Done deal.

God loves you and has always been inviting you, as you are, into *shalom*. Inviting you, as you are, out of the wreckage and into a new beginning of life and love and beauty and wholeness and completeness and harmony. Inviting you, as you are, into the full immersion of an entirely different present reality. And God is speaking your name to let you know that you have always been loved as you are, that you have always been worthy as you are, and that in this embrace of the Divine you are being made whole.

I rarely say this, but when I do you know I mean it. Praise God!

RETHINKING THE
FORGIVENESS OF GOD

Let's talk about forgiveness. You may have always thought of forgiveness as a verbal sentiment only given when an adequate measure of contrition, remorse, or tears have been poured out. And that is completely understandable, because that is the model of forgiveness we have been culturally-conditioned to understand, especially in our churches. Within that model, forgiveness is conditionally given in exchange for a person being sorry for their sins. The key word is *conditionally.*

It usually plays out something like this. God has the power to forgive you or to not forgive you. And God's forgiveness will absolutely not be given unless you are really sorry for what you have done and then go through all the right steps to show how sorry you are.

But interestingly, what we find in Scripture is actually something very different than the conditional, reactive forgiveness that holds power over people.

In story after story, and account after account, we discover that the forgiveness of God, demonstrated through the life and teachings of Jesus, is *unconditional* and *preemptive*. It happens before any of us acknowledge it or do anything to receive it.

God's forgiveness is always unmerited and given before anyone ever asks for it.

There is absolutely nothing anyone can do to earn that kind of forgiveness, because it is birthed out of compassion and mercy and is given regardless of one being sorry.

But many miss God's unconditional, preemptive forgiveness because they project their merit-based forgiveness system on to God and then look at the Bible as a mechanical process to be exactly followed or as a mathematical equation that only equals forgiveness if all of the numbers are added up correctly.

The forgiveness of God is not based upon merit and is neither a mechanical process to follow, nor a mathematical equation to get correct, in order to receive it.

God's forgiveness is completely one-sided and was demonstrated at the cross of Christ for all people, for all time. In every way the religious have believed, or continue to believe, that non-stop sacrifices, penance, or daily words of contrition are necessary on our part to be at peace with an angry, temperamental god, it was God who finally put those faulty assumptions to rest, once and for all, by offering a peace sacrifice *to us*, not continually expecting sacrifices *from us*.

Stop and think about that for a moment.

It was God that made a peace offering to us, in Jesus, to prove that there is absolutely no hostility or anger toward us. There is only a longing to be at peace with us and then to be in relationship with us. And in any way we have rebelled from that peace and relationship, it has already been forgiven.

So rather than an authoritarian power play that holds forgiveness or unforgiveness over our heads until we are contrite and remorseful enough, or until we have offered enough sacrifices, or until we have shed enough tears, the forgiveness of God stands alone. It has never been dependent upon any single person climbing the ladder of worthiness or attaining higher levels on the fictitious relative sin scale. It is unconditionally and preemptively self-giving and self-generative, and birthed out of God's great compassion and mercy *for all of us*.

And as a result, there is only and always forgiveness for all equally and the hope of a restored relationship.

A MOVEMENT TOWARD RELATIONSHIP

God's forgiveness has always been God's first move toward restoring a relationship with each of us. And if you have missed that then you have missed the entire point.

The forgiveness of God allows for the repairing and mending work in our relationship to begin. For the two to become one. For that which has been divided to come back together. For that which has been in disunion to be reunited. For wholeness, completeness, and harmony to be realized in our relationship. That is precisely what reconciliation is. It is the process that slowly begins to build trust, heal wounds and divisions, and make relationships whole again over time.

And that is the hope of God. That in light of God's forgiveness, our relationship will be reconciled, will be made whole and complete, will move toward perfect harmony, and *shalom* will be realized in and through our lives.

Interestingly, that is why followers of Jesus are referred to as *ministers of reconciliation*, rather than *ministers of forgiveness*.[8] Because God's forgiveness has already been given to all. That is the Good News. And now, in light of God's forgiveness for all people, we are those who announce to the world that there is no enmity, hostility, or condemnation from God toward anyone.

There is only love and forgiveness and open arms that welcomes back every prodigal.

BREAKING INTO WHAT IS ALREADY THERE

I want to share something very eye opening and mind-blowing with you.

On the day of Pentecost, Peter is preaching to the crowd and says, "Repent and be baptized, every one of you, in the name of Jesus Christ *for* the forgiveness of your sins."

From the outside looking in, it sounds like Peter is telling the people that in order to be forgiven, they must first repent and be baptized and then, and only then, will they be forgiven by God.

And that is the way countless Christians have taken that verse over the centuries. It is viewed as a conditional transaction between God and a person. In essence, the forgiveness of God will only be given *when* you say the right words, when you have a repentant heart, and when you are baptized in the water.

But here is the crazy part.

In that verse spoken by Peter, the word translated as *for* is the Greek word *eis*.

Eis means *a motion into, penetration, union.*[9]

So what many have always read as this conditional transaction between people and God is actually a movement we make into something that is already there, something that has already been given, something that already surrounds us. And that something… is the forgiveness of God.

We don't do something for God's forgiveness. We move into, and find union with, a forgiveness that already surrounds us.

And our faithful acts of repentance and baptism are those movements we make that penetrate into, and find union with, that forgiveness that was given long ago.

God's forgiveness is not being withheld like a stingy miser. Nor is it dependent upon you being good or perfect, or going through the right steps. God's forgiveness is already here. It has already been extended to all. It is all around you. The invitation into forgiveness and a life of *shalom* was given long ago. All you have to do is enter into it.

And no one can keep you from entering, as you are.

WHY DOES THIS MATTER?

The reason this matters is because we ultimately extend that which we believe has been extended to us. And as long as we believe that God only forgives those who ask for it, those who deserve it, and those who are repentant, then we will do the same with others.

This is single-handedly the most important reason for us to understand that God's forgiveness is unconditional and preemptive, because it truly affects how we view and treat other people.

For instance, if my sister was sideways with my dad, but he already unconditionally and preemptively forgave her, what right would I have in continuing to finger point, accuse, and hold it against my sister?

Since my father had already forgiven her, ought it not change how I see my sister (as forgiven)? Ought it not open my eyes to see how I am not in a position to accuse, condemn, or be hostile toward her? Ought it not cause me to be as forgiving toward her as my father?

Understanding God's forgiveness is not a matter of subtle nuance or simply a chicken and egg discussion without any real world practical consequence. This distinction matters so much right now.

It matters for how Christians view and then treat other people, especially the LGBTQ community, drug addicts and abusers, the homeless, those who are in our country illegally, and any other group that is being judged and marginalized.

IT'S SO GOOD TO BE ALIVE

To be really blunt here, it has never been more important than it is today to abandon self-limiting, self-assured religion and discover life in the *shalom* of God.

Because when we are immersed into the radical forgiveness and inclusion of the Divine, we are surrounded by the very heart of God, which has always been an unconditional, self-sacrificing, other-centered love. And when we penetrate head-first into the forgiveness and lovingkindness of God, we begin to change at the heart level and it changes how we see other people and how we experience this life in all of its brilliance and fullness. In this intimate, relational union with God, we actually begin to become like our Father.

God's unconditional love becomes our unconditional love.

So what you may have never tasted in the past, or what you may have only tasted in part for a fleeting moment in the past, has now become a life overflowing in abundance in this present moment.

But this time.

It's here with us in every present moment moving forward. Heaven birthed within us, no longer as fleeting, transient moments that slip through our fingers, but as our new way of living, as a newborn, as a new creation, as a little child, with new eyes, a new heart, and breathing as if for the very first time.

It is so good to be alive again. And this is what God wants for us all.

But unless we become like little children, unless we are born again, unless we seek after and discover this new reality, we will never see or experience the kingdom of God in this life. We will never discover anything outside the limitations of religion. We will never move beyond our disunion with the Divine, nor enter into the present union of *shalom.*

But when we do, we carry this new life with us into every experience. This peace and forgiveness within our souls begins to flow into our every interaction and conversation and relationship. This joy in our being begins to delight in the resident goodness of all things- every sight, every sound, every touch, and every scent. And this deep love in our hearts begins to awaken us to a beauty in all things that we may have previously missed or taken for granted.

Like sitting in silence and meditating and praying and communing in the life-giving presence of God. Taking an early morning walk and contemplating the beauty of creation and giving thanks for all that we awake to every morning. Sitting down for a meal with our families and friends each evening after a long day. Seeing every person as a brother or sister who is unconditionally loved. Hugging the brokenhearted, sharing words of life and encouragement to those who are having a hard time, or making a meal for the family who lost a loved one. Serving meals and sitting at a table in conversation with those who gather at the hot meal site. Visiting and caring for the widow in our neighborhoods. Holding the hand of our spouse during their chemotherapy treatment. Remembering all of those moments in our lives and cherishing them and giving thanks for it all.

It's every single moment of our lives, even in the hardship, even in the pain, even in the wreckage where heaven and earth come together, where a new reality births within us and we begin to see and experience all things differently.

And that is so much more than religion could ever give you.

BUT YOU ARE PRIVILEGED!

There may be an urge to believe that this kind of experience is only for those who live and exist within a place of privilege, but let me disabuse you of this thinking.

The present experience of *shalom* makes no distinction based upon life situation.

Everyone, in every life situation or circumstance, has equal access to it. But for some, it's easier to find than for others. For millennia, those who have been in the *least privileged* of life situations were actually those who had easier access to the *shalom* of God, while those in the *most privileged* of life situations have had more difficulty finding it. This is what Jesus means when he says that, "It is easier for a camel to go through the eye of a needle than for someone who is rich to enter the kingdom of God."[10] When one believes they have everything they need, there is a tendency for them to also believe that they do not need anything else to fulfill them. But when one realizes the poverty of their life, there is a great desire to search for that which gives in abundance.

But it is available to all who seek after it, equally.

Even Paul, imprisoned when writing a letter to the Philippian church noted:

I have learned to be content [and self-sufficient through Christ, satisfied to the point where I am not disturbed or uneasy] regardless of my circumstances. I know how to get along and live humbly [in difficult times], and I also know how to enjoy abundance and live in prosperity. In any and every circumstance I have learned the secret [of facing life], whether well-fed or going hungry, whether having an abundance or being in need. I can do all things [which He has called me to do] through Him who strengthens and empowers me [to fulfill His purpose—I am self-sufficient in Christ's sufficiency; I am ready for anything and equal to anything through Him who infuses me with inner strength and confident peace.][11]

That is why it is not based upon life situation and why it is freely available to all and why no one can keep you from entering into it. Because it is free to all who hunger and thirst for it. And there is not one religious person or leader who can stand in the way of you entering. There is not one religious leader who can decide whether you are in or out. There is not one religious leader who can keep you from a seat at this table.

The religious may stand on the outside and try to close the door, and prevent you from entering with rules and methodologies and classes and expectations, but Jesus opens wide the door and invites us all to a seat at the table with him, without judgment or condemnation.

So no matter your background, your present life situation, your socioeconomic status, your level of education, your appearance, your diseases, your addictions, your afflictions, your offenses, your burdens, your heartache, your despair, or even your past or present sins, there is no single person, not one religious person, not one holier-than-thou person, not even the most theologically-minded, well-respected, or studied preacher who can keep you from this embrace, who can block this perfect love and perfect freedom, or who can take away your seat at the table of invitation.

As followers of Jesus, we have not been given the task of shutting the door or preventing "sinners" from entering into the Kingdom of God.

Rather, we have been given the task of entering presently through the open doors ourselves and then accompanying every single person of the world to the table so that they, too, can taste and see just how good the Lord is.

The kingdom of God is not a place that needs guarded or protected. It's not a place entered into by the self-described righteous or religious. And it is certainly not a place where the untouchables, outcasts, or unholy sinners are banned or restricted.

The kingdom of God is here. It is present. It is all around us and surrounding us and just waiting for us to see it and discover it and receive it. And this is the only place where the wholeness, completeness, and harmony of *shalom* if found.

The door is always open. There is always a seat at the table.

You have been invited, as you are.

QUESTIONS

1. What is unhealthy religion and what does it look like for individuals, relationships, communities, and the larger world? How is unhealthy religion so detrimental to *shalom*?

2. What is a healthy religion and how can it be a catalyst for people to experience and then extend *shalom* into relationships, communities, and the larger world? What would that begin to look like?

3. What was the biggest surprise or revelation you uncovered in this chapter and why?

4. In your own words, how would you describe *shalom*?

5. How is it that *shalom* can be experienced despite the life situation or circumstance in which one finds him or herself?

CHAPTER 4

A More Beautiful Suffering

So may the sunrise bring hope where it once was forgotten.

SAM BEAM

*Make way for the heart of love that leads
us through the path of suffering.*

JOHN LUCAS

I have begun the process of changing my mind about birds. And that is a big deal for me.

Those closest to me know that I have this unreasonable phobia of the feathered friend. It has something to do with a mother bird dive-bombing my head to protect her nest when I was five. And no, to answer your question, I was not bothering her nest. I was simply going next door to a friend's house. But, there is no reasoning with a mother bird.

Anyway, my neurosis aside, I am slowly taking steps at rediscovering the beauty (or some redeeming quality) of birds.

An Indiana winter can be brutal and bone-chilling. And it is not made any more bearable by the local meteorologists who giddily, and a bit too affectionately, begin referring to it as a Polar Vortex. The tragedy is they don't realize that by calling it a "Polar Vortex," it psychologically becomes twenty degrees colder. So let's just be honest here. We do not need "Polar" anything in Indiana, especially when it is already pitch black at 4pm in the middle of December.

But there was a moment a few years ago in late winter, when darkness still owned the morning and the cold refused to let go of everything in its grip, that I heard the sweetest song.

Through the shroud of night, before the sun's first rays, amid the polar chill, a melody of hopeful anticipation pierced the dark veil of winter and announced that spring would soon be arriving.

It was glorious and profound.

The processional of spring, a time of life, new beginnings, and spectacular beauty was coming! And it was being ushered in through song by feathered vocalists announcing it's arrival.

I, a crusty-eyed morning zombie of multi-layered, nighttime attire (pre-coffee), could not miss this staggering metaphor.

LIVING IN PAIN AND SUFFERING

When a season of darkness surrounds us and seems as if it will last forever, we may very well begin to believe that this is the way life will always be. But even in the darkness, if we are still enough to hear it and patient enough to trust it, there is always the sweet song of the Spirit, leading us in hopeful anticipation, surprising us with beauty in the present, and giving us a glimpse of the life that's yet to come.

I know it is terribly difficult to discuss how we can learn to see beauty amidst the wreckage when we are in the throes of a painful life situation, whether it be temporary or permanent. But, it is in this place where we must always begin, in the place of our pain, in the place of our suffering. For it is in those places where we can, mostly easily, lose heart, feel completely lost, grow wildly cynical, and begin to blame God for our condition or circumstance.

Even more, our pain and suffering can easily become the place from where we begin to live our lives.

The crushing weight of our suffering will always try to convince us that the pain we are experiencing is our only reality and that there is nothing redeemable there, ever. And as a result, the pain we are experiencing can begin to manifest outwardly in our lives through our words and actions, ultimately affecting how we see the world and how we relate to others. It can make us angry, bitter, resentful, and hard-hearted.

That is what suffering can do. It can cause us to reside in our pain, no matter how great or small that pain is, and then become the lens through which we begin to see people, situations, and the world as a whole. And over time, our pain through suffering can very easily spiral downward and lead to questions and then to the destruction of our identity, our worth, and our purpose in life.

MY OWN WOUND

A couple of years ago I interviewed to take my boss' job when he left our company. He and I had been connected at the hip for over two years and I was incredibly fortunate and grateful that he had subsequently endorsed me and advocated on my behalf to take his position. Additionally, throughout the hiring process, I had eight hour long interviews and hit grand slams with each of them. I had even asked each interviewer to make me their top candidate, to which all but one person agreed to do. I felt incredibly confident that the position was mine to lose.

But when the decision was ultimately made.

I didn't get it.

And I was completely and utterly devastated. I mean it thoroughly wounded me.

I don't pour my heart and soul into many things, but I had poured my heart and soul into this. And not getting the position wrecked me.

I'm not trying to be super melodramatic here. This is what I really felt on the inside. And it was hard to not feel it on a moment by moment basis. Even worse, it was hard to not live out of the wound and the pain I was experiencing.

I'm not sure if you have ever lived out of a wound, but let me tell you, it is a place of death.

It is angry.

It is bitter.

It is hateful.

It is prideful.

It is toxic.

And it makes you all of the things you were never created to be.

The truth is that the easiest thing in the world to do is ignore the wound and the pain and let it fester. And I promise you, it will ultimately become the source from which you begin to live your life. The toxicity and infection will spread and manifest in how you see people and situations, how you relate to others, and in the words you use and the actions you take.

A neglected and infected wound is toxic and leads to death.

And I am ashamed to say, that was me.

Not too long ago I was talking to a friend with whom I talk every day. While I came into the new year resolved to mentally move forward from not getting the new position, there was still a lot of hostility in my words that came from my deep wound. My head was saying that it was time to let the healing begin, but my wound disagreed. And it was unfortunately winning the battle of my heart.

That's when my friend said something to me that made me stop in my tracks.

He was like, "Outside of work you have so much peace, but at work, you really have a lot of anger."

I knew he was right, but it was so hard to hear, so hard to admit.

While I had been trying to mentally move forward, I had buried my deep and concealed wound and was living out of it. And while it was full of death and completely toxic, I had never taken time to face it, to introspect, to pray over it, and open myself up to get the necessary healing and restoration that I so desperately needed. I had just tried to ignore it and move on, but it was there the whole time killing me and infecting everyone around me.

It's easy to get into a place where we selectively introspect. But we all have blind spots. And if I had not been pushed by my friend, I would have never been forced to look inwardly, to ask where this death was coming from, or to come face to face with my wound.

The truth about myself was that I had a painful wound and I had been living out of it for over a year. And it did not begin to heal until I humbly faced it and asked God to join me in that place of pain and suffering.

END DESTINATION OR TRANSFORMATIVE PASSAGEWAY

Living constantly in the pain of our suffering can either become an end destination or a passageway for each of us.

As an end destination, the pain of our suffering can become a place where we stay in bitterness, sadness, anger, hatred, resentment, and unforgiveness.

As a passageway, our pain through suffering can become the pathway to profound life transformation and to new ways of seeing and experiencing the world.

Suffering breaks us down into insufferable little parts where we can either self-destruct or cry out helplessly to God, because we are in a place where we have seemingly lost control. Our sense of self has been shattered. Our identity has been obliterated. And it is in our place of pain through suffering where we can choose whether we make it our final destination or a transformative passageway.

That is the profound mystery of suffering. Suffering strips away any and all control we believed we had over people and situations. And it is in this place, our place of suffering, the place where we have lost all control, where our hearts and minds can either be closed off or open to the healing and transformative love and *shalom* of God.

And no matter who you are or what you have been through or are currently going through, you can choose what you want to do with your pain, and how you receive suffering. You can let it dominate and control how you see the world and relate to others, or you can use it as a means to be taught and guided into a new and more beautiful way of living.

THE SLIDING SCALE OF SUFFERING

But let's be honest, no matter how our sufferings may be used as a means to guide us into a more beautiful way of living, no one prefers to suffer.

Our natural inclination is to avoid painful life situations or circumstances that lead to any sort of suffering. And consequently, as a culture, we have been on a long trajectory toward avoiding pain and seeking escape from any sort of mental discomfort. And what we now consider suffering has dramatically shifted. What may have been viewed as a simple inconvenience, or as the natural consequence of living in an earlier time, has shifted on a relative scale from inconveniences to suffering.

If our internet service goes down, we believe we are suffering. If we keep score at our kid's game and there is a loser, we believe we are suffering. If we don't have options for every dietary restriction or preference, we believe we are suffering. If someone disagrees with us or doesn't like our opinion, we believe we are suffering. If we don't get the latest iPhone, we believe we are suffering.

I want to make sure I am clear on this point.

I don't discount the fact that a person may truly believe they are experiencing some sort of suffering in those instances, but our sliding scale of suffering has significantly shifted. We now have a lower threshold for what causes us to suffer.

But it is not as if any one of the examples above independently led to this shift. It has been the slow aggregation and evolution of how we perceive and internalize inconveniences, and all those things that cause us mental discomfort, which has led us to this point.

What ought to be regarded as small bumps in the rugged road of life have now come to be perceived and internalized as pain and suffering.

And being that our perception of what constitutes pain and suffering has changed, deeply traumatic circumstances will inevitably put us into territory we have never previously traveled and could very easily lead us to pursue means that alleviate the pain, that numbs our suffering.

That is where we are today as a culture.

I know this is a broad stroke of the brush and that this does not apply to all people, but we are largely a people who cannot cope. We are a people who do not know how to enter into our suffering and face it and hold the tension of it. We are people who have a low tolerance of pain and, as a result, use whatever means is at our disposal to avoid it. We do not see our pain through suffering as a transformative passageway. We see it as an end destination of wreckage and devastation that must be avoided because there is nothing redeeming or beautiful that could ever take root and grow in such darkness. So we seek to alleviate our pain and numb our suffering by any means necessary, whether it is through ignoring and suppressing the pain, which festers and infects. Or, through entertainment, gaming, eating, illicit drugs, and alcohol, all of which simply helps numb the pain and temporarily escape it, but never heals the wound.

And this avoidance, this numbing, this escape comes at a great cost to us individually, relationally, and even communally.

This is not a judgment. It has been true for me as well.

SUFFERING AS A BEGINNING

The reason I am going to such lengths to describe how our collective consciousness has evolved on the relative suffering scale is for this reason. I believe that if we have a hard time coping with those things that were once regarded as "simple inconveniences" or those things that cause a "mental discomfort," we will not have the mental, emotional, or psychological capacity to deal with more deeply traumatic or extreme circumstances when we face them.

And as a result, our pain and suffering will certainly become an end destination from which we live an infected, toxic life, rather than the transformative passageway through which we grow and experience a deeper, more abundant life.

Even more, in our pain and suffering as an end destination, we will not know how to walk alongside others who are going through their own traumatic circumstances, or how to develop deeply-rooted and intimately connected, nourishing relationships with others who are suffering in their isolation, if all we do is run from and avoid our own pain and suffering.

There is a line of wisdom in the letter written to the church in Rome in which Apostle Paul writes that, "suffering produces perseverance, perseverance creates character, and character leads to hope."[1]

In this line of wisdom, suffering is never an end destination. It is just the beginning. Suffering is the fertile ground upon which something beautiful can begin to grow. It is the place where we learn to persevere, where we develop a depth of character, and where there is a strengthening in our understanding of how to be a community that suffers alongside one another in hope.

And as hard as this may be for you, this is one place where we learn to find beauty in the wreckage of our pain and suffering.

BEAUTY CAN COME FROM THE WRECKAGE

I often think about the grief my grandparents experienced when an aunt I never knew died as a one month old baby to whooping cough.

The anticipation of pregnancy.

The joy of a new arrival.

The excitement of each new day with their baby.

But then.

The grief of losing their newborn.

The sadness of what could have been.

The despair that accompanied each passing day.

After Judy's death, my grandparents visited the cemetery each Sunday. It just so happened that the cemetery was next to a church. And while my grandparents were not people of faith, the church family would join my grandparents in their pain and suffering, comforting them, consoling them, and walking alongside them in their loss.

Through their loving kindness and compassion, my grandparents began to follow Jesus.

And I have to tell you, this story tears me up everytime I share it, because my grandparents were not planning to have any more kids once Judy was born. But as a result of her premature and terrible death, they decided to have one more child.

That child was my dad.

And through this strange paradox, I am only here on this earth, very literally, because Judy died as a one month old baby.

It is tragic and horrible and beautiful. But these are the tensions we hold together right now.

Let me be clear. God did not make her die. God did not need another angel. God wasn't testing anyone's faith. God didn't have a better plan for her. God was not sitting on high like a grand marionette orchestrating this death for some greater good.

We live in a world that is suffering under the weight of immense pain and suffering and death in the present. But even in our pain, even through our suffering, even in the throes of death, God is there with us, surrounding us, holding us, hurting with us, grieving with us. And even in the most painful and horrific situations, God can still bring healing, still bring life, still bring transformation, and still bring hope.

God does not cause death, but can bring life and beauty from it.

For all the pain my grandparents experienced. For all of their sufferings. For all of their grieving tears and burdened, sleepless nights and heartaches, did they know that I would be sitting here, writing these words of life and love and beauty and hope to each one of you?

And is it possible that those same eyes that once shed tears of sadness on the broken, yet fertile ground will one day shed tears of joy for the seeds I have planted in that ground?

Is it possible that their days of great loss and great sorrow can be redeemed, at least in a small way, through a lifetime of gratitude, joy, and blessing that I experience and pass on to others?

Is it possible that a young life did not pass away in vain but can be honored with what I do with my life, how I live it, and how I pass it on?

Beauty can, and will, come from this wreckage and devastation. But sometimes, it may not be apparent to you, or even apparent to you in your lifetime.

Suffering, as an end destination, is nothing but wreckage and devastation and hopelessness. It is a wasteland where nothing good is found and where misery and brokenness reside. It is the valley of the shadow of death.

But suffering, as a transformative passageway, is the ground upon which beauty flourishes, where hope is birthed. It is the morning light, the dawning of a new day, from which the first hopeful rays break over the distant horizon of the valley that causes the darkness to flee.

You may not trust these words right now, but there is hope in your pain and suffering.

From the outside looking in, pain and suffering as a transformative passageway where beauty begins to spring forth, is completely counterintuitive. It is upside-down thinking to the logical mind. But for the contemplative seeker, for the humble mystic, it is the power of God that brings life from death.

Again, it's not that we actively seek out painful situations, or enjoy our sufferings. We don't. Suffering is a natural inevitability of this life experience that we all will face and enter into at some point in our lives.

But there is an awareness and trust that begins to develop within the contemplative seeker and the humble mystic in understanding that no matter the degree or type of suffering we are experiencing, there is something beautiful at the core of our being, at the very center of our humanity, being birthed deep within us, that can transform our pain and suffering into something extraordinarily beautiful over time. We are being forged with a depth and resilience into something invaluable and useful and magnificent, even when we don't see it or trust it, when we are willing to face our pain and walk headfirst into our suffering, in a posture of humility, that leans into the Spirit.

For it is in this place where transformation begins, both within us and then ultimately through us for the benefit of others.

QUESTIONS

1. Think of a time when you experienced a painful life situation in which it became an end destination for you and then the place from which you began to live your life. What were the feelings and emotions you experienced in that place? How did it affect your attitude and relationships?

2. Think of a time when you experienced a painful life situation in which it became a passageway to life transformation. How did it change you? How did it change the way you see the world and how relate to the people around you?

3. Why do you think it is so much easier for a painful life situation, or suffering, to become an end destination rather than a passageway leading to life transformation?

4. What pain are you currently holding, or suffering that you are currently enduring, that you have been choosing not to face? What would a first step look like for you to begin moving out of that end destination? What fears do you have in taking that first step?

5. Could you ever envision a time when your experience journeying and transforming through pain and suffering could be used for the benefit of others going through a similar situation? If so, what would that look like?

CHAPTER 5

The Possibility of Joy

*Not surrendering to melancholy is the most
important thing, if you are going to fight your
way out of whatever corner you are in.*

BONO

I have heard many people say over the years that our lives are like icebergs. In fact, my brother-in-law has a tattoo of an iceberg on his forearm, which reminds me of this premise every time I see him. His tattoo is accompanied with the words, "I am not an island. I am an iceberg." The implication being that there is so much more to him than what you see on the surface. There is a depth below the surface that many people may not even realize.

To me, the image of an iceberg is so evocative. There is this massive, colossal behemoth, floating in the water, of which only ten percent is ever visible to the naked eye, while the other ninety percent remains hidden or unseen.

Like each of our lives.

There is so much more below the surface of one's life, so much more at the depths of one's being, than anything we will ever see on the surface.

And this may be true for you at this exact moment.

You may be trying your best to put a smile on your face and hold it together when you are around other people. You may be trying to pull up your bootstraps each morning and keep your routine so that you don't draw the attention of family and friends. You may be trying to do your very best to look composed in front of everyone who sees you, as if everything is okay in your life.

But down deep in your heart and soul, below the surface where no one else can see, you are aching.

Maybe you have lost a child, a parent, a friend, or a pet this year. Maybe you have been diagnosed with a terminal illness or know someone who has been. Maybe you are dealing with and carrying regret for relationships that have been destroyed because of your words or actions. Maybe you are lost and alone and don't have anyone standing next to you, holding you up, or giving you the strength to carry on. Maybe you are holding on to disappointments and failures and wondering if you have any worth, value, or dignity remaining. Maybe you have had a miscarriage or had difficulty getting pregnant. Maybe you have lost a job, hate your job, and are struggling to provide or find a new way forward. Maybe you have reached the height of success but still feel empty inside and without purpose. Maybe you have hurt your friends and your family and you feel as if you can never be forgiven. Maybe your marriage is on the rocks, or in complete shambles, and you just don't know how, or if, the pieces can ever be put back together.

Maybe, maybe, maybe.

And simply having a perspective that your pain and suffering can either be an *end destination* or a *transformative passageway* does not necessarily produce a whole and healed heart that no longer aches, that no longer groans.

It is the hardest thing to hear someone say that your pain can be a *transformative passageway* when there is no end in sight to it.

I understand. I have been there myself.

But we always have a choice as to whether we stay wounded, crushed, and broken in our suffering as an *end destination*, or if we ultimately face our pain through suffering and let it be the beginning place of transformation and beauty.

For if we are to begin this upward ascent from the valley of the shadow of death, it begins with the acknowledgement that we do not want to stay in this place forever. And it may help you to know that this journey does not require you to leave your aching heart behind.

The end destination for a wounded and broken heart is never the valley of the shadow of death. We carry this wounded and broken heart with us, upward over the mountain. And we carry it together, brother. We carry it together, sister.

The truth is that your pain and suffering can be a transformative passageway *even while* your heart aches, *even while* your spirit groans.

It just requires that we begin this journey together with a humble and open heart.

DON'T GIVE UP

Somehow there has been this unrealistic idea invented within religion, either intentionally or unintentionally, that living in our sufferings and carrying a broken heart is incompatible with experiencing life transformation or living a full, abundant life. We have been led to believe that it is an either/or proposition, because there is no way a person can be transformed by the

Spirit, used by God, or experience an abundant and overflowing life presently while we are still aching and groaning.

That is absolutely not true.

Even though we presently ache and groan from the wreckage around us and carry our wounded and broken hearts with us, it is still possible to enter the sweet embrace of heaven and earth, to experience perfect freedom and perfect love, to experience joy and an abundant life.

I know this may sound impossible or contradictory to what you have ever been taught or told, but it's the truth.

Likely the most influential biblical passage for me over the last decade comes, again, from the letter written by Paul to the church in Rome. It is an astonishingly beautiful passage in the way he describes the difficulty and pain of this present life, while also detailing a creation that is pregnant with new life and hope.

> All around us we observe a pregnant creation. The difficult times of pain throughout the world are simply birth pangs. But it's not only around us; it's within us. The Spirit of God is arousing us within. We're also feeling the birth pangs. These sterile and barren bodies of ours are yearning for full deliverance. That is why waiting does not diminish us, any more than waiting diminishes a pregnant mother. We are enlarged in the waiting. We, of course, don't see what is enlarging us. But the longer we wait, the larger we become, and the more joyful our expectancy.

> Meanwhile, the moment we get tired in the waiting, God's Spirit is right alongside helping us along. If we don't know how or what to pray, it doesn't matter. The Spirit does our praying in and for us, making prayer out of our wordless sighs, our aching groans. The Spirit knows us far better than we know ourselves, knows our pregnant condition, and keeps us present before God. That's why we can be so sure that every detail in our lives of love for God is worked into something good.[1]

Right in the middle of the wreckage and pain and suffering that is all around us, and that we presently carry within us, a new life of *shalom* has been conceived and is growing within each one of us. And this new life is growing as we eagerly and expectantly and joyfully anticipate the birth of this new creation in fullness in the future. So while we hold together the tension of our pain and our new life of *shalom* within us, we look forward in hope to a time when all will be made right.

It is like a mother who experiences the increasingly intense and powerful pains of pregnancy for nine months leading up to the birth of her baby, yet who is infinitely, immeasurably, inexhaustibly joyful in her anticipation. In the same way, we literally hold within us the tension of our groaning, our pain, and our suffering together with a new life that has been birthed within us.

And we are presently, expectantly, and longingly joyful.

That for which we hope to arrive in its fullness one day, is within us right now. And it is holding us in our heartache. It is groaning with us in our suffering. It is praying for us in our weakness. And it keeps us in the presence and communion of the Divine even when we don't have the words.[2]

That is why I would encourage you to never give up no matter how difficult life may get. That is why I would encourage you to never stop believing that there is so much good left in this life. That is why I would encourage you to never believe the lies that your pain and suffering has to remain an end destination of your life, or that the only way forward is to leave your broken heart behind, or that you should feel guilty experiencing happiness or joy while carrying your broken heart with you.

You do not have to resign yourself to a life of infinite sadness.

Because there is still so much beauty that surrounds you. There is the sweet embrace of heaven and earth that is holding you and comforting you and that is all around you. There is the overwhelming and all-consuming love of the Spirit that envelops you and that groans with you and that prays intimately for you. And there is the joyful love that is birthing and growing within you, that you can feel right now, and that sustains you in your pain, even while you are longingly expectant.

I felt this tension powerfully last year at the end of October. I received a heartbreaking text message from my work partner, whom I had been partners with for the last eight years, telling me that she had one to two months to live. She was a breast cancer survivor and had been cancer-free for the last five years. And inexplicably, it came back with a vengeance, in her lungs, liver, and brain. I came home and sat on my back porch and cried. Tears were streaming down my face. I was heartbroken.

And as I looked up, I saw my six-year old little boy, Will, with his full Spiderman costume on, running around the yard, jumping and landing like Spiderman, and then pretending to shoot his web. It was the funniest thing to see him playing by himself and using his imagination and having so much fun. Even with the pain and tears and heartache of that moment, there was still so much beauty and joy.

I sat there with a smile and many tears, holding the tension of the two.

And we do not have to feel guilty for holding this tension. We can hold and carry our pain and suffering with us while bearing witness to all that is good in this life.

OUR WORST DAY

I know that my words can often drift so far into poetic imagery that it may feel as if I have abandoned a real and raw practicality for an unrealistic idealism. But like the mighty and colossal iceberg, there is always so much more below the surface that you can't see. My words on these pages are just the tip of the iceberg that rises above the surface of the water that you can see clearly. But below the surface, in the depths where no one can see, is my own broken heart.

While the last year has been difficult for my family and friends, on so many fronts, nothing could have prepared us for what happened one night in late February of last year.

My house church is a group of my best and closest friends who have gathered together in our home for the last twelve years. On any given Monday evening our house is packed with twelve adults and fifteen kids, three of them now in college, ranging in age from a newborn to twenty years old. We are one big family that has been through the highest highs and the lowest lows together. And the love we have for one another has been strengthened through every single experience we have shared.

I love my friends with all of my heart.

It's not uncommon for us to have a text message thread constantly running that includes almost everyone in our group. Many times our messages are about what food someone is bringing when we gather together, crazy emojis or GIFs to celebrate a birthday or a special occasion, or sharing about someone who needs prayer. It gets crazier than that (boom), but you get the general idea.

One Saturday night I sent a text to the group discussing plans for a massive celebration and feast that we would be having on the upcoming Monday. We had been doing a 13-week study on 1st Corinthians, that had actually taken 70-weeks to finish (more on this in Chapter 9), and we were ready to let our hair down and have a serious blowout.

But within minutes of my initial text to everyone, the message thread would be completely turned upside-down. We received a text from Jackie about Abbott, her fifteen-year old son. He was being life-lined to a hospital in Indianapolis due to a tragic accident.

I can't even begin to explain how everything changed for each one of us in that moment.

Abbott and two of his good friends had just finished playing basketball on an unseasonably warm, early Spring evening. As they left the park and drove for a few miles, they decided to pull over on a side street a couple of miles from the courts to dry off and change clothes. The details of what happened next are not essential for this story, but in the next few moments after the boys pulled over to change clothes, two of the boys got back in the vehicle and accidentally ran over Abbott.

We were with Adam, Jackie, and their daughter Ella at the trauma center when the trauma team came into the room and told us the news that they could not save Abbott.

It was the worst day of our lives.

There are no words.

There are simply no words.

We stayed at the hospital for hours that felt like years and then ended up at Adam and Jackie's home early the next morning. Family and friends began to arrive carrying both food and broken hearts. And it wasn't just Adam and Jackie's friends and family that showed up at their home. It was all of Abbott's friends as well. They came by the carload.

While it was amazing to see all of these students arriving at the house that February morning, there was something else happening that was even more unimaginable. As the kids came into the house, Adam and Jackie told them to let Abbott's two best friends, who were with him on that fateful Saturday night, know that they, too, were welcome to come to their home.

And it wasn't long before each boy showed up.

It was both the most heart-wrenching and beautiful thing I have ever seen in my life.

The boys cried as they came into house and said, "I am sorry. I am sorry. I am so sorry."

Without a single moment of hesitation or judgment or animosity, Adam and Jackie embraced each boy and held them in grace and mercy and forgiveness and said, "It was an accident. Abbott loved you. And we love you."

In my four decades of living, I have never seen the love of Christ more sacrificially demonstrated than in those moments. I stood there with tears streaming down my face. They were tears of grief and pain. They were tears of profound sadness for Adam, Jackie and Ella. They were tears of profound empathy for Abbott's friends.

But they were also tears of God's overwhelming and fully enveloping love that held Adam and Jackie and that was expressed through them as they held each boy in that moment.

A person could hear a thousand sermons, spend a lifetime studying the Bible, and yet never see the sweet embrace of heaven and earth, the enveloping and all-consuming love of God, so clearly, so perfectly embodied as it was in my dear friends in that moment.

Amid the horrific and unimaginable tragedy, the earth-shattering heartache, the devastation of complete wreckage, there was a beauty that defied all logic, that defied every human sensibility.

And every single person in that place on that day was a witness to it.

We felt it holding us. It was sustaining us in our utter brokenness. And that indescribable beauty, that glorious beauty, surrounded every one of us. But it was because of Adam and Jackie, even in their incomprehensible, unimaginable pain and suffering, that this magnificent beauty was welcomed into that place, at that moment.

And it is specifically because of how they chose to bless when it would have been easier to curse, of how they chose to forgive when it would have been easier to blame, of how they chose to love when it would have been easier to hate that we still see the concentric waves of that beauty washing over us more than a year later.

But the pain of that fateful day still feels like it was yesterday.

It's not as if a turn of the calendar page erases the heaviness of a heart, or takes away the burdened weight that one carries. It's not even as if the welcoming of a new year can reset your mind or help you forget the previous.

The days come and go.

The weeks accumulate.

Yet the heartache remains.

›Our groaning does not understand time.

Our pain does not end with the calendar year.

Our suffering does not dissipate with the passing days.

It is real yesterday, today, and tomorrow. It is here and here and here, moment by moment, and has no regard for imaginary and illusory divisions of time, nor does it wane with the opening of gifts or with yuletide cheer, nor is it convinced to subside with New Year's resolutions.

Our groaning, our pain, our suffering has no regard for hours, days, weeks, months, years, centuries, or millennia. We carry it with us everywhere we go.

So while we may have been witnesses to indescribable beauty, to a moment when heaven and earth literally came together, right in the middle of so much pain and suffering, and even while we still feel the waves of it washing over us, is it even possible to believe that we can enter into the *shalom* of the Divine while we still hurt? Is it even possible to believe that we can experience life to the fullest, life in all of its abundance, not just in fleeting moments, but each moment of the day while still carrying this heartache? Is it too unrealistic to believe that there is any more beauty to discover and receive in this wreckage?

IS JOY AN IMPOSSIBILITY?

I sent a text to Jackie and asked her those same questions before they left as a family for a camping trip to Arkansas during Thanksgiving. She said that she would need some time to think about the questions and that she would take some notes while they were gone.

Here is what she gave to me on a piece of paper a few weeks later:

> Losing my son has made me feel the biggest, darkest, most searing pain I have ever experienced in my lifetime. It is an unfathomable black hole. The pain does not dissipate on a daily basis. It is still there. But it hides in little nooks and crannies. It shows up when least expected. And when it does, it literally feels like a huge, gaping hole is being pulled from my chest, right at my heart center. My breath leaves my being and it takes everything I have to find it again. The pain creeps through my body and it wells up through my throat and to my head. There is nowhere for this pain to go. Sometimes it seeps out of my eyes and I have a good cleansing cry. Sometimes the pain turns to anger and I get extremely mad that I no longer have him with me, in the physical. Sometimes the pain turns into an extreme darkness, sadness. This is a place where I can not cry. Wishing I could. Willing myself to do so. This is the place where I want to hide in my own head in distraction.

I have to explain this extreme pain before I can explain the beauty I have seen and felt ever since our tragedy.

There are so many moments and I won't be able to explain them all. But there are moments of pure comfort. I can feel Abbott's presence, and it is beautiful, and comforting. I have to quiet my mind for only a short time and I know he is here with me.

Before Abbott was gone, but while we were at the hospital, waiting to hear the terrible news, our family came. And I am not talking about my immediate family. We have the closest Divine-given family, whom we have already been through hell with, and we didn't know they would be with us at 11pm that night, an hour away from home. But during this dark moment, where time is still and all you have is prayer, I looked up and here they came walking toward us. I know this may sound weird, but there was an inexplicable feeling. The way they were walking toward us, together banded-in-arms. They looked like troops, the kind that fight for all that is good. This was the first most beautiful experience. And they haven't left our side all of these months. They continue to lift us and carry us.

Our friends have shared their hearts with us. People we have never met have sent letters, texts, hugs, and encouragement. We have even shared tears with them. The outpouring of love comes from every direction. We feel as if we are being carried in arms we can't see. I still hear children say prayers for us and Abbott. I see teenagers show huge signs of love. I can be such a cynic of human behavior, but this is just the outer edge of how amazing people have been to us.

Then there are the signs from God proving he is with us, that he is with me. The simplicity of being in nature and feeling the warmth of the sun on my face, on my back. The quiet in the mountains, the rustling of leaves in the trees. The breeze in the air meeting the wind chimes. The richness of the earth. The colors. The smells. The laughter of my daughter. The embrace of my husband. I just have to stop to notice it.

There is a stark contrast between the pain and the beauty of this life. I have to know when to stop looking in the mirror so I can see outside myself. When I turn my attention away from me, the beauty is so evident.

There is a beauty that pierces through the thin veil where heaven and earth come together. It is a present taste of that which will be fully and completely realized in the future. And when we enter into that space, it is an awakening to the resident goodness of all things. It is *shalom*. It is the experience of pure joy. You can see it. You can feel it. You can hear it. You can taste it. And you know it is good. And you long for it, not in fleeting, transient moments, but in perpetuity, even when carrying immense pain.

It is sitting down for that first cup of coffee in the morning, smelling it, tasting it, savoring it. It is every delicate cut of the onion, celery, carrots and the deeply satisfying aroma of the earthy spices when making soup in the cold of winter while the delicate snowflakes fall outside and the fire's warmth radiates around you. It is walking outside on an autumn evening when you close your eyes and breathe deep the magnificent fall fragrance. It is closing your eyes while being enveloped and suspended by your favorite song, noticing every harmony, every note, every melody. It is sitting around a table with your best friends with great food getting lost in conversation. It is holding your baby, hugging your children, the touch of your spouse, and the embrace of your mom and dad while you savor every moment. It is a loving church community surrounding parents who just lost their baby. It is watching your son run around the yard in his Spiderman costume and shoot webs. It is embracing and holding two teenage boys in grace and forgiveness and unconditional love.

And it is remembering every good and perfect moment and longing for them once again.

That is *shalom*. That is eternal life now. That is the experience of pure joy. That is the beginning point of learning to see beauty in the wreckage. That is the ever-present gift of now, an eternal present receiving that we can embody and experience despite our changing life conditions or our painful sufferings. But it is also the deepest unsatisfied longing of our souls.

We presently receive, but expectantly and longingly anticipate.

Every feeling, every touch, every song, every embrace, every memory, every unsatisfied longing will be satisfied one day. Every terrible wrong will be made right. Every deep wound will be healed. Every crushing heartache will be comforted. Every painful tear will be wiped away.

It is, and it will be, a great joy for all the people.

But that for which we hope to arrive in its fullness one day, is within us right now. And it is holding us in our heartache. It is groaning with us in our suffering. It is praying for us in our weakness. And it keeps us in the presence and communion of the Divine.

QUESTIONS

1. Why do you think it may be difficult for a person, who is going through a painful life experience, trauma, or suffering, to believe that it can be a passageway to life transformation?

2. Why do you think the idea that "living in our sufferings and carrying a broken heart" is believed to be
incompatible with experiencing life transformation or
living a full, abundant life?

3. If a person does not have to leave behind their broken
heart in order to begin the journey of allowing their
pain and suffering to be a catalyst of life transformation, what possibilities does this open for a person's
life?

4. Think of a time when, even in your pain and suffering, you were still able to see or experience beauty?

5. What does a person risk losing by becoming consumed and enveloped in their pain and suffering?
How might this impact, not only their individual
well-being, but also their relationships with others
and their contribution in the community at large?

CHAPTER 6

Prayer as Breathing

And you fill me with your breath. And
you make me breathe again.

MANY ROOMS

Despair no more and use this breath to pray, to pray, to pray.

LATIFAH ALATTAS OF PAGE CXVI, SONG *I LOVE*
THE LORD ON *LENT TO MAUNDY THURSDAY*

Ancient cultures believed that there was a sacredness in breathing, a sacredness in each person's inhaling and exhaling. Jewish sages and scholars intimated that the sacred name of God, YHWH, could be heard with every exhalation of breath.

So it was, in our first breath of life, YHWH breathed life and his name into our lungs. And with every subsequent breath, in each of our lives, as we exhale, the sacred name of God is spoken.

Whether this is true or not is inconsequential, but it speaks to an incredible intimacy between the created and the Creator.

It is amazing how involuntary our breathing can become. Breathing is an autonomic function of the body that does not require our attention, unless we are intentional with giving it our attention. We can go days or weeks or maybe even months without ever thinking about our breathing, about our inhaling and exhaling, which I believe is an incredibly revealing and enlightening truth about our lives.

Our lives can become so involuntary, so mechanical that we do not recognize the sacredness that we breathe in moment by moment. Our lives can become so busy and loud and chaotic that we are not able to hear YHWH when we breathe.

It's no accident that in a letter to the church in Ephesus, Paul writes that they should *pray at all times in the spirit.*[1] At first glance, that line may read more churchy than mystical, but there is a breadth in the original Greek that we so easily miss in our English translations that actually brings it to life.

The verse reads pray in the *pneuma.*

The Greek word *pneuma* means *spirit, wind,* or *breath.*[2] And to me, this paints an absolutely beautiful picture of prayer and intimacy with the Divine. As with every breath we take, prayer becomes our natural rhythm, our moment by moment eternal present receiving and giving, our inhalation and exhalation of the sacred and holy.

Prayer is our most primitive and essential act of being. For in our prayer as breathing, we strip away all that we have accumulated, release all that has shackled, and clear all that has clouded. Prayer as breathing is a centering and then a receiving of the present moment. And it is in this place where we can once again begin to hear YHWH with every inhalation and exhalation.

THE STRUGGLE OF PRAYER

But if you are anything like me, you may struggle with prayer.

Prayer has always been portrayed by our culture, or taught by our churches, as this redundant and repetitive exercise before meals and before bed, or a ritual undertaken during a church service, in which we ask God for things and then thank God for what we have.

I am not pointing fingers here.

In many ways, my wife and I have had this regular, repetitive rhythm with our kids when we pray with one another each day.

And insofar as it goes, there is really nothing wrong with offering our petitions and thanksgiving to God in a regular daily rhythm.

However, the issue is when that becomes the final destination of our prayer lives. And for many, that is the final destination. It is a place where we only pray to God as a genie, of sorts, or who we go to in order to ask for those things we want. It is a place where we only pray to God as a blessing machine who needs to be thanked for all that God "gives us," or where the depth of our prayer lives can only be measured in singular, finite moments before a meal or before bed.

That is not God's intention with prayer- to be a genie who grants our every wish and desire, to be viewed as a blessing generator who only offers goods and services for our consumption, or to only be addressed at fixed times throughout the day.

God's intention with prayer is union and constant communion with us.

PRAYER AS BREATHING

But once again, there is a significant limitation in our translation from Greek to English.

There is only one word for the word prayer in the English language. And that word is… *prayer*. So when a person mentions the word prayer, one immediately thinks of folded hands, bowed heads, and words spoken to God.

However, an interesting thing begins to happen when you look at the original Greek word. What you quickly find is that there are dozens of descriptive words used for prayer in the original language, each meaning something slightly different from the others.

But the Greek word used in the *pray in the spirit* verse referenced earlier is actually the most all-encompassing word for prayer in the entire Bible. It is the big dog of all prayer words, if you will.

The word is *proseuchomai.*

Proseuchomai doesn't just capture one single element or aspect of prayer. *Proseuchomai* captures every single element, variation, and aspect of prayer. *Proseuchomai* is prayer that encapsulates surrender, words of confession, words of humble request, prayers made on behalf of others, and words of praise and thanksgiving.

So to *proseuchomai in the pneuma* means to surrender with every breath. It means to confess with every breath. It means to make humble requests with every breath. It means to offer prayerful words on behalf of others with every breath. And it means to give praise and thanks with every breath.

That is what Paul means in another letter when he writes to *pray without ceasing.*

As we breathe, our lives become a prayer that never ceases. It is the place in the Spirit where we live, we move, and have our being. It is the beginning place of our union and constant communion with the Divine. It is the beginning place of the sweet embrace of heaven and earth coming together within us with every present inhalation and exhalation. It is the beginning place of this ever-present receiving of *shalom*.

Our prayer as breathing is the invitation of shalom.

And there is an absolutely beautiful intimacy in giving everything we have and everything we are to the Divine- every thought, every emotion, every motive, every heartache, every burden, every tear, every praise, and every word of thanksgiving, always done with every breath taken.

In *proseuchomai*, we do not find a distant god removed from our lives or a god who only wants our prayers a couple of times a day or a god who simply wants our wish lists or a god who just wants to hand out blessings to us.

Instead, we find a God who wants us to come close, intimately close, and to bring it all, everything we have, everything we are, in constant and continual communion, fully present and fully alive, with every single breath we take, and share our heartaches, our struggles, our hardships, our burdens, our insecurities, our requests, our celebrations.

But at times, it takes us removing ourselves from everything so that we may find the space to rediscover our breathing, to pay attention to what we are feeling and to what we have been carrying, so that we may offer it to God and receive something new in its place.

That is the beauty of prayer as breathing, or centering prayer. In this very intentional act of contemplation, which some may refer to as introspection or self-examination. We look inwardly to discover all that is keeping us from receiving *shalom*, so that we may call it by name and give it to the Divine.

RELEASE / RECEIVE

It may be doubt or frustration with God about your life situation. It may be the guilt you have been carrying for talking poorly to others about your best friend. It may be the resentment you have been harboring for the promotion you didn't get at work or for the stress and strain from the high expectations put upon you by your parents, friends, or work colleagues. It may be the deep and heavy sorrow that is weighing you down and causing your life to spiral out of control. It may be those things you keep hidden from everyone, but that you deal with daily.

Every thought that is keeping you from *shalom*.
Every feeling that is keeping you from *shalom*.
Every heartache that is keeping you from *shalom*.
Every burden that is keeping you from *shalom*.
Every resentment that is keeping you from *shalom*.
Breathe it out.
Find peace in giving it to the Divine.
And as you breathe in, listen. This is your eternal present receiving.

What is the Divine speaking into you? Do you hear your name? Do you hear that you are worthy and valuable? Do you hear that you are fully and unconditionally loved as you are? What is God giving you in this very moment? Do you feel the peace? Are you experiencing healing? Are you surrounded by a loving presence? Are you receiving new eyes to see the world, a new way of living and relating to others, a new found freedom and love you have never known, the courage to make amends with those you have hurt or wounded, the peace to deal with all of the anxiety that is surrounding you and weighing you down, or the humble power to forgive a person who has wronged you?

This is where *shalom* begins. Breathe it in.

And in a very real way, this is the power of the cross and the power of the resurrection, but again, don't get lost in the heavy religious imagery or the negative baggage that the cross has amassed over the centuries.

The cross of the Christ is almost exclusively discussed as an event with only cosmic or supernatural implications, but having no real bearing on one's present life, or no real practical application in one's daily routine. It is the narrow notion that God did something *for us* on the cross, but that the cross has no real impact on us when we wake up in the morning and go about our day.

You may hear people say things like, "Jesus died on the cross to save me from my sins," which basically means that God did something supernaturally that spiritually took away their sins and saved them.

And while I don't want to discount that assertion, the cross has unfortunately become *only* symbolic of what God had to do to fix the problem of our sin, while we have no responsibility whatsoever.

However, if we understand sin as our disunion from God, then the power of the cross to defeat sin is that which brings us back into relational union, or *shalom*, with God.

So not only is the cross where we discover the true heart and character of God demonstrated in the crucified Christ, it is also the place where we too personally sacrifice, or crucify, all that has kept us from being in perfect relational union, perfect *shalom*, with God.

The power of the cross is not some cosmic, unilateral transaction done by God to magically erase our spiritual sins that are floating around somewhere in the cosmos, so that we can say, "My sins have been taken away, hallelujah!"

The power of the cross is mutual self-emptying.

The power of the cross is mutual self-giving.

The power of the cross is mutual self-sacrifice.

The power of the cross is the defeat of sin, or our disunion with God.

The power of the cross is the union of Divinity and our humanity.

The power of the cross is *shalom*.

It is the discovery that the true heart and character of God has always been a self-emptying, self-giving, self-sacrificing love. And the way we come to embody that same self-giving, self-sacrificing love is by picking up our own cross daily and crucifying those things that keep us from entering into the *shalom* of God.

And that sacrificial act begins in our prayer as breathing, in what we are breathing out, in what we are giving, in what we are releasing, in what we are crucifying in prayer to the Divine, and then in what we are receiving from the Divine as we inhale the breath of new life, as we inhale resurrection, as we inhale shalom.

Let everything that has breath praise the Lord.

WE DON'T STOP

For what we are facing in this world, it is essential that we find our breath, that we discover space for centering, contemplative prayer.

Because the pace at which we are moving is increasing without any evidence of slowing down. The amount of information coming at us at any one moment is doubling and tripling in the wrong direction. The degree to which we are connected to technology only promises to make us more connected and more connected, not less. And the accumulation and strain of our stressors and burdens continue to be bottled up inside of us without any means of decompression or release.

It feels like suffocation or drowning or losing control or all of them at the same time. And this feeling, this state of being, is now shockingly normal because we have not known any other way.

Generation after generation has passed and we have evolved into a culture that does not stop, that does not rest, that does not take time to breathe, that is losing its heart, and that does not understand our desperate need for breathing as prayer. Even more, we are an increasingly rationalistic culture that views this eternal present receiving, this communion with the Divine, this internal presence of the Spirit, as archaic and optional, at best, or foolish and silly, at worst.

In many ways, we are existing as wayfarers and travelers, without even the faintest memory of how we once entered this world, naked and free, with only *YHWH* in our first full-throated breath.

How desperately we need to rediscover that place again.

How desperately we need to be naked and free once again.

How desperately we need come out from behind the figurative fig leaf and be reunited with the Divine.

And it is evident.

In our anxiety.

In our stress.

In our mania.

There is no denying that we are paying for it heavily with our hearts, our minds, our bodies, and our souls. And these forces keep coming. They continue to increase in their depth of intrusion and distraction. And they keep taking more of us and more of us. It may be subtle, but it is incremental and completely overwhelming, stretching us to a near breaking point.

THE MOST AMAZING STORY

That is the place where my friend Jackie was about four months after Abbott died, as she was preparing for a backpacking trip to the Pacific Northwest with a couple of her friends. Jackie knew, both literally and figuratively, that she desperately needed a retreat and to take the first steps out of the valley if she was ever going to begin the slow ascent up the mountain.

While she did not share with us everything she was thinking as the trip approached, one thing she did share was that she needed to go out into nature and just breathe and decompress and find peace and stillness after Abbott's death. Unbeknownst to us at the time, Jackie was also going on this trip to give her pain to God and to ask for a sign that God was with her in this place of pain, to know that God had not abandoned her.

Being that she was going to be in one of the most rainy regions of the United States, she simply asked God to give her a rainbow as a sign that she was not alone and that God was with her through this tragedy.

On the last rainy evening, utterly dejected, having not seen a rainbow over the three previous days, Jackie said that she "had words with God," and that, in her brokenness, she was "washing her hands of God."

She poured out her heart and soul to God in agony, simply seeking God's presence, seeking communion with the Divine, in this place. She broke herself open in real and raw and unfiltered emotion to God by saying, "I have lost my son and I am broken and in so much pain… and the least you could do is let me know that you are with me in this. But you can't even do that. I am fucking done with you."

The next morning, as the sun came up against a promising blue morning sky, the ladies broke camp and were met by a husband and wife team who would be shuttling them back to the ferry. They loaded their gear into the flatbed truck and took their spots amongst the gear.

As the truck barreled down the road, Jackie, who had recently gotten a couple of tattoos after Abbott died, noticed that the lady in the passenger seat also had a tattoo on her forearm, but couldn't quite make out what is was or what it said. It wasn't long before the truck drove onto the ferry for the short ride out of the National Park.

As they reached the other side and began to unload their gear, the man, whom the ladies affectionately referred to as "Standing Rock" (because of his imposing stature), and his wife got out of the truck and joined the ladies to help them with their gear.

Jackie noticed that Standing Rock had a tattoo of baby's foot on the back of his leg with a date just below the tattoo.

It was Abbott's birthday.

July 9th.

Shocked and taken aback that he had a tattoo with Abbott's exact birth date on his leg, Jackie pointed it out to her friends.

Among the surprise and chatter, Standing Rock's wife explained that their newborn baby boy died on that date, so they each got a tattoo to commemorate his life. Moved by their story of loss, Jackie told them that Abbott died four months earlier and the date of their tattoos was Abbott's birthday.

July 9th.

And that's when the lady walked up and turned over her arm to show Jackie her tattoo.

There is a rainbow
of hope at the end
of every storm
7-9-16

There are just no words.
The rainbow.
The date.
The promise.
Never will I leave you.
Never will I forsake you.
Breathe deep, for I AM here.

I don't share this story with you as a promise that you will have some sort of miraculous encounter with God in your pain and suffering. That's not my intention at all.

I share this with you as a perfect example of what it looks like to *proseuchomai* in the *pneuma*, to find retreat from the forces that are bent on suffocating us, drowning us, or causing us to lose control. This is what it looks like to sacrificially give everything we have and everything we are in an unceasing, unbroken prayer to God with every emotion, every feeling, every heartache, every tear, and with every single breathe. And this is what it is like to desperately seek union and communion with the Divine and to discover the eternal present receiving of life in the Spirit. For even in our utter brokenness, the love of God does not abandon us, but envelops us, as we breathe deep this *shalom*.

Learning to see beauty in the wreckage is not an intellectual pursuit that is undertaken by thinking and willing ourselves out of distraction and suffocation. It is an exercise of contemplation, of introspection, of learning how to breath by exhaling our heartaches, our struggles, our hardships, our burdens, our insecurities, our requests, and our celebrations. And then, breathing in deeply to inhale and receive, and then become, the *shalom* of God.

QUESTIONS

1. What is your traditional understanding of prayer? In what ways has your traditional understanding of prayer been good for you? In what ways has your traditional understanding of prayer been bad for you?

2. In what ways can prayer as breathing begin to, "strip away all that we have accumulated, release all that has shackled, and clear all that has clouded?"

3. Why do you think God's intention with prayer is union and communion? What would be the benefit of that for human beings? How is this different than what you previously believed is God's intention for prayer?

4. What does prayer as breathing reveal to us about the nature and character of God? How is this different than what you previously believed about the nature and character of God?

5. How does the imagery of the cross and resurrection become the form and shape of contemplative, centering prayer?

CHAPTER 7

Shalom as Transformation

*Broken people, we can be made whole, we can
be made whole, we can be made whole.*

THE BRILLIANCE

Over the last decade I have written over a quarter million words. I have written on hundreds of topics, some encouraging, some hopeful, some beautiful, some prophetic, and some that were very, very difficult or emotional. My prayer has always been that my words would be written only in love, and written only in hope of us becoming the kind of people, together, that we were always meant to be.

That has always been my heart and prayer, but that has also been the unfortunate paradox of my own life experience.

Over the last couple of years I had become incredibly discouraged with writing, but not necessarily discouraged with what I was writing. I was frequently lost in my head, coming back to the same horrible, lingering questions after every writing endeavor that would hang over me like a dark, heavy cloud.

Why do I waste my time writing when no one seems to care? Why do I spend so much time writing when nothing ever seems to change? Why do I painstakingly labor over these words and try to find creative ways of expressing them, when it seems to be such a monumental waste of effort?

I know these are terrible questions and I feel horrible that I, not only entertained them, but also began answering them in ways that suggested I actually believed my words were a waste of time and effort.

And to be honest, this kind of vulnerability is hard to share with you. Not only does it reveal how unhealthy my thinking was about myself and about my writing, which I actually love to do with all of my heart, but it also reveals how incredibly judgmental I can be toward others when I don't see the kind of change I expect in their lives and relationships.

There's my confession.

As one who is always standing in the gap between *what is* and *what could be*, who is always pushing and calling others to something greater beyond ourselves, and who is always trying to see the possibilities of a better future, when I begin to live in a way that makes *me* the center, while resisting the *shalom* of God, I become increasingly frustrated, self-righteous, and judgmental of others. And as a result, I begin to believe this false narrative and begin to live out of this lie.

MOVEMENTS

It's crazy the paths we travel and how easily we can end up believing so many lies about ourselves and other people. They are lies that actually begin to creep into our hearts and minds, and then manifest in our lives, as a result of our disunion from life in the Divine.

We can travel so far away from who we were always meant to be and how we were meant to experience this amazing life.

But here's the truth.

There is an individually unique way in which each of us were created to be. There are beautifully diverse ways in which we are all wired. But in our movements away from *shalom*, we can very easily forget who we are and, instead, begin to reside in and live out of our disunion.

And any movement away from Life in the Divine is a movement toward death.

Death in how we begin to think.

Death in how we begin to live.

Death in how we begin to relate to others.

Since God is Life, the One in whom we live and move and have our being, then any movement away from this Life in God is a movement toward death. It is really that simple. And it is this death that begins to manifest in our thinking and then outward in our actions, in our relationships, and into our world.

Jesus says it this way, "I am the Vine, you are the branches. When you're joined with me and I with you, the relation is intimate and organic, the harvest is sure to be abundant. Separated, you can't produce a thing."[1]

Our relational disconnection from God is the beginning point of every lie, every antagonism, every injustice, every oppression, every hatred, every animosity, every unhealthy motive, and every fractured relationship.

And in this relational disconnection from God, we begin to live in fear and lies and pain, which then causes us to live in unhealthy ways to protect our ego, or our false self, that we have created. In our relational disunion, our false self is at the very center and we do everything we can to protect it, preserve it, indulge it, and justify it, which can lead to an increasingly unhealthy existence.

And in me, it was this persistent internal narrative that convinced me of the lie that my frustrations of people and situations were justified. But here is the really difficult part. As I reflected on this lie, I began to realize something even greater about myself. Dissatisfaction and resentment have been the recurring themes of my entire life. And my writing was just another place to be embittered in frustration and to reside in resentment.

When you are living in the lie, you can't see how distorted your thinking truly is or how far from *shalom* you have strayed.

I truly believed that the worth and value of my writing was correlated with the number of people who read it, who agreed with it, how many "likes" I got on social media, and then by how much it changed the people who read it.

It was a completely self-centered way of thinking that set me up for perpetual anger and resentment, that then robbed me of the profound joy and serenity of being able to simply express myself through words and the honor of being able to selflessly share what I write with others, whether it be one person or a million, whether it gets a "like" or a "love," or whether it changes the world or not.

That's what happens when we move away from *shalom*, we each undertake an endless search on a winding road to discover worth, value, identity, purpose, and love that can then be easily misdirected toward those things that can never give us what we truly long for. We will be forever searching, but never finding. We will be endlessly disappointed and disillusioned, and always longing for a deeper fulfillment in our souls.

For me, as a writer, I was seeking approval and notoriety from others and was endlessly disappointed and disillusioned, angry and resentful.

However, in union with the Divine, in the *shalom* of God, like a light being carried into the darkness, we begin to see the lies we each have believed about ourselves and then begin to uncover the disillusionment through which we have been living.

And it is here, in this place, where we at last discover that the true heart of God has always been an unconditional love. And this unconditional love is the singular source of our worth and value. It is the only true source of joy and happiness. The only place where we find our life's fulfillment. And that is enough.

What a beautiful, beautiful relationship.

SEE DIFFERENTLY, BE DIFFERENTLY

It was this message of *shalom*, and then the experience of *shalom*, that ultimately transformed my head and my heart. I was taken from a place of anger and resentment toward others, to a place of unconditional grace and love and peace toward others, and to a place of freedom and joy in my life.

But this transformation, this inner holy work of *shalom*, began with a very simple parable.

There is a parable that Jesus shared with a huge crowd. It was of a farmer who sowed seeds that fell on various types of ground. Maybe you have heard this one before. Some seeds fell along the path and birds came along and quickly ate them. Some seeds fell in rocky places where they sprang up rapidly, but could not take root, so they withered and died. Some seeds fell on shallow soil and the sun easily scorched them. But there were other seeds that fell on good, rich, fertile soil, that then took root, and produced even more than what was originally sown.[2]

The way we have always understood that parable, maybe even the way I have always taught that parable, is that we need to be the type of people whose lives are like the good, rich, fertile soil, ready to receive the seeds of *shalom* sown by God, so that they may take root and produce fruit in our lives. And that interpretation is absolutely true.

But there are always more perspectives and more messages in parables that are not always readily apparent. And it was this other perspective that obliterated the lie I had believed about my writing and other people.

In addition to becoming a fertile soil, I realized that I am also the farmer who has the good pleasure of freely and liberally sowing the seeds of *shalom* that have been planted within me, everywhere I go. It is not my responsibility to worry about where the seeds fall or if they shrivel and die or if they actually take root and begin to grow. My only preoccupation is to wake up each day, grab the bag of seeds, and joyfully sow everywhere I go. And it is my good pleasure to continue scattering and spreading the seeds of *shalom*, this good news of *shalom* in the Divine, among each of you everyday with the words I speak, with the words I write, and the life I live.

What is freely given to me, I continue to freely give. And there is a profound joy in that place of shalom.

That is where my joy was rediscovered and my purpose reignited. I was being transformed and was experiencing a love and a freedom in my life that I had only previously experienced in those rare moments throughout my life when heaven and earth seemed to come together.

But it was here again and it was changing me to *see differently*, to *be differently*.

PERSPECTIVE IN RAIN

I had recently been walking around in the rain on a 41-degree February work day. It was the kind of day when the rain would just. not. stop. And to be honest, I had not really thought that much about the cold and rain throughout the day. With my job, I am in and out of offices all day and I have gotten used to the wildly variable Indiana weather. But as I was nearing the end of the workday, I walked out of the last office and directly into the pouring rain toward my car.

In that split second, I almost grumbled in frustration about the cold and wet.

But I caught myself.

I'm always amazed at how many thoughts and questions can go through a person's head in just a fraction of second.

Why am I getting frustrated?

Why am I getting frustrated with the rain and cold?

Why am I getting frustrated when I will be in my car in 15 seconds?

The quick succession of questions immediately took me back to one of the most emotionally difficult days on our 2014 Alaskan backpacking trek from Stony Creek to the Toklat River in Denali National Park. It was our third day and we were covering eight-miles of rough terrain, all without trails, fighting miles of alder and tussock. The rain was unrelenting, as it pounded us in the cool 40-degree wind. There was not a single dry place along the entire route for a short reprieve, not even for a short, dry lunch break. We were in the unforgiving heart of Alaska, out in the wide open, completely exposed to the elements. And we had to deal with it, because there wasn't anywhere else to go.

I snapped back into the present, still walking through the parking lot. That quick memory of Alaska made me smile. And within seconds I was laughing audibly, like a crazy man who had just lost his mind, thinking of my relatively insignificant present inconvenience. The joy of unlocking my door, getting into my dry car, and turning on the heat eviscerated my frustration before it could even be birthed. I was immediately thankful.

So why in the world did I spend so much time sharing these stories of my frustration, my anger, and my resentment with you?

MY TRANSFORMATION

You may think they are fairly innocuous compared to the deeper issues and problems each of us face every day. I mean, come on, was it really a huge win to not be frustrated by people not "liking" or "loving" my writings on Facebook? Was it really a life accomplishment to not be frustrated by a little rain and cold at the end of the workday?

I completely get it.

But I have to tell you, it goes so much deeper than that for me. I have always lived a very reactionary life, in which my automatic internal frustration gauge was always set to maximum. And while many people may have never seen my frustrations visibly, they were always there raging within me. I leaned heavily toward frustration and anger when my circumstances were not ideal. Words like self-reflection or contemplation were not a part of my vocabulary, let alone a regular rhythm of my life.

And it all came to the surface one day while talking with my boss when we were talking about my last seventeen years with the company. In this crazy moment of complete honesty I blurted out, "The last seventeen years with this company can be summarized as frustrating."

What did I just say? Not only could I not believe I said that out loud, I couldn't believe I was being so brutally honest about myself.

And sadly, as I thought even more about it, I realized that I have been frustrated for the last *twenty-five years* with disappointment after disappointment, resentment after resentment, frustration after frustration.

The even harder truth to admit is that I resided in a relatively joyless existence for the majority of my adult life. I was always frustrated with my own personal situations and with the people around me, whom I believed were making my life difficult. And it didn't help that during much of this time, I was addicted to news and politics, which was a lethal cocktail for that much more frustration. It was an exhausting existence to always be frustrated or angry or outraged about something or someone. And it was starving me from living this life in fullness and abundance and joy.

Even more, when anyone would confront me on the absence of joy in my life, I would summarily dismiss the assertion, or perceived accusation, by claiming that I was using my cynicism in a positive way. The truth is that I was a joyless person hiding behind pretense and justification. And that is the ideal place for an egocentric man to hide and remain unchanged. My resistance and excuse-making were the perfect ingredients for an unhappy, unhealthy, and stagnant life. And the ideal facade to keep my false self intact.

So while it would be easy to dismiss my stories of rediscovering joy in my writing, and then laughing like a wild man as the rain poured down on me in a parking lot, to me they represent a man who has been slowly changing and patiently transforming into someone more content and joyful, and hopefully, someone growing more beautiful each day. They represent a man who resisted *shalom*, but then learned the hard way that there is a greater peace and joy and contentment in this life when I find my worth and value and purpose in relational union with God. It is in *shalom* alone where we find life. There is no other place.

Here's the truth. When we find space for self-reflection and contemplation, we begin to see ourselves more clearly, maybe even for the first time. And in all the ways we have propped up, defended, and preserved our false self, allowing space for self-reflection and contemplation can begin to change us into something new and even more beautiful.

That is what the holy inner work of *shalom* begins to do in each of us. It frees you to become your very best self, the self you were always meant to be from the very foundations of creation, the self that is wholly and completely loved, as you are, by God.

And that is the most beautiful and liberating thing in the world.

Maybe you are like me, a person living each day, veering further and further from your true self, spiraling in disunion, longing for a life that isn't so angry, so disappointed, so hopeless. Maybe you have spent the majority of your life in constant, maybe increasing, frustration with the small irritants of your daily life. Maybe this constant frustration has accumulated over the years and has been robbing you of joy and the experience of beauty and magnificence and wonder that surrounds you and envelops you. Maybe your frustrations and irritations have hardened you through the years, disabling you from recognizing the small miracles and beauty of every seemingly ordinary moment.

Maybe you have been experiencing pain or carrying a heavy burden with you each day as you walk out the door. Maybe you are in a place where you are depressed, where you feel worthless, or in a place where you are living in constant shame. Maybe you wake up each morning grieving your life, thinking about the life you used to have, and living in remorse for what you have lost or how you have pushed others away. Maybe you hate yourself, hate what you have become, and you know that you are about to hit rock bottom.

Only you know exactly what you are dealing with or going through.

NOT A 5-STEP PROGRAM

It's at this point where it would just be easier to tell you exactly how to fix your life, or to tell you what steps you need to take to experience the transformation of *shalom*. And that is the leaning of so many self-help books and so many faith communities. We live in a "quick fix" culture with neither the time, nor patience, nor capacity for a space of contemplation, self-reflection, or seeking.

Think about it this.

Even the central elements of Christianity, the bread and the wine which represent the Body of the Christ and the Blood of the Christ, which is also ironically referred to as *Communion*, has become more of an express task to quickly check off the church service to-do list, rather than liminal space for contemplation, self-reflection, and the seeking of *true communion* with the Divine. Some may say that we simply don't have the time during a church service for creating that kind of space. But maybe that is the central issue endemic within churches and in our lives. We simply reinforce the character and proclivities of our culture, rather than guide others into a new way of experiencing and living this life.

And that seems shockingly opposite from Jesus.

I am always struck by how evasive and non-specific Jesus was when he spoke to the crowds of people who followed him around and listened to his teachings.

In fact, in the parable of the sower referenced earlier, the disciples actually went up to Jesus after he shared that parable with the audience and asked, "Why do you speak to the people in parables?"[3]

In the disciples I hear a sense of frustration like, "Why don't you just tell them what you want them to do? Just tell them what they need to do to fix their problems, rather than being so frustratingly ambiguous with them!"

But what we find from Jesus is that he is not interested in giving people the Five Easy Steps to Shalom, as much as he is interested in a people who continually seek to find it for themselves.

And when he responded to the disciples he said the reason he speaks to the people in parables is because they don't have the eyes to see or the ears to hear and understand the deeper truths and mysteries of this life. In other words, since they don't get it, he doesn't take the time to explain it to them, because they are not seeking anything deeper.

Again, like a treasure in a field that is hidden, so is *shalom*. It isn't found by simply showing up and then consuming what you have been fed. It is only found by those who actively seek after it, who hunger for the deeper treasures of this life. And this may give us insight into why so many people within churches remain untransformed. We have created consumers, rather than seekers. We have created a culture of fill-in-the-blanks, rather than a culture of searching the mysteries of this life. We have created a culture of quick fixes, rather than a culture of contemplation.

I recently went to a Celebrate Recovery Impact Night in which seven individuals shared their stories of addiction and recovery. It was an absolutely, mind-blowingly beautiful night. There were seven stories of men and women who had lived in lies, neglect, addiction, anger, hatred, depression, guilt, and grief. The common theme with each story was that when they "hit rock bottom" they had to come face-to-face with whom they had become and how their addiction destroyed their lives, families, friendships, and careers.

When a person finds that space of self-reflection and contemplation, or that space where we are able to see ourselves clearly, whether it be through our own choosing or forced upon us by hitting rock bottom, it is in that place where everything we had previously built up, or hid behind, comes crashing down, leaving us totally naked and exposed.

But it is also that place where a new life can be constructed. It is a place where pretense, justification, and lies are obliterated and where we can begin to see clearly the life and beauty of *shalom* in the Divine. That's why it is easier for those who have lost everything to find the Christ, because everything in which they had previously trusted has been obliterated, has failed them, and is now gone. There is nothing left to hold on to, except the Christ, and that is where Life is ultimately found. That is why privilege means nothing for discovering *life to the fullest.*

The truth is that we desperately need more churches that look like Celebrate Recovery groups, because we each long to be liberated from that which is consuming us, controlling us, addicting us, rather than hiding behind the masks that we put on week after week, acting like life is perfect, yet remaining sadly untransformed.

HOLY INNER WORK

As we have discovered, this movement from disunion to union, this movement into *shalom* with God, is a movement into the forgiveness of God that has always been right in front of us, inviting us in.

And while our breathing as prayer is a sacrificial discipline that invites the *shalom* of God to come intimately close, as we discussed in the previous chapter, it is only when we begin to live and reside in that place that we begin to experience transformation.

Shalom is where the holy inner work begins. It is the light that exposes the darkness of our false self and the love that resurrects and illuminates our true self.

And this movement from the false self, which exists in disunion, toward the true self, which is resurrected in *shalom*, is a holy (and wholly) transformative experience. It is the discovery of, and the transformative movement toward, who we were always meant to be as fully integrated, fully alive human beings.

RETHINKING REPENTANCE

There's a chance you are wondering what in the world I am talking about, or maybe you are scratching your head trying to figure out what all of this means and how it relates to my story above and to your own life.

There is a word that occurs regularly throughout the New Testament that is so much richer, with so much more depth than the way it was translated into English and then the way we have come to understand it. The Greek word is *metanoia*, which is usually translated into English as *repentance*.

For me, the word *repentance* conjures up so many negative images. I think of the old time preachers with a Bible in one hand, shaking it at the audience, telling them to, "Repent or go to hell!" Or, those who stand on the street corners today and berate every single passerby to repent or pay the eternal price. Ironically, I have been the victim of both the old time preachers and those who stand on the street corners. And if I am being really honest here, I had grown to hate that word. It always felt like this terrible threat that should scare me, and others, into a "saving relationship with God," which I thought was weird. On the one hand you have the God-man, Jesus, instructing us to love our enemies, to do good to those persecute us, to bless those who curse us, to go the extra mile, to turn the other cheek, and to give the shirt off our backs to our enemies, yet who is ready to throw us in to hellfire for not "repenting."

But the more I came to know and fall in love with the Jesus of the Gospels, I wondered where all of the vitriol and anger toward his audience was. I wondered where the threatening message of "Repent or go to hell" was. I wondered why he didn't shake his King James Bible at lost people or pound his fist in outrage at the "terrible sinners" or stand on the street corners railing at unworthy heathens.

I began to discover that there was a Jesus that didn't look anything like the "Repent or go to hell" preachers of my past, or the hateful, venomous street preachers that we deal with today. And that takes me back to this little word *repentance* that everyone has grown to despise.

As you can probably imagine, there is a real life context that surrounds words and that gives them so much more meaning than their simple definition.

The same is true for the Greek word *metanoia*. There is a cultural context surrounding that word that may help us understand it even better.

In Greek mythology, *Kairos* was the god of *opportunity* portrayed as a man with winged-feet who was always on tiptoe, indicating constant movement, and adorned with a long, single lock of hair that extended from an otherwise bald head. It was understood that as *Kairos*, or *opportunity*, passed by, there was a fleeting moment in which one could seize *Kairos* by the lock of hair before the moment, or *opportunity*, passed.[4]

Obviously, the deeper meaning was to *seize the opportunity* at the right moment before it was lost, or before it passed.

However, when opportunity was missed, a shadowy, cloaked goddess named *Metanoia* stood in the wake of the missed opportunity. *Metanoia* symbolized the regret of missing the opportunity at the right moment. But there was also something more that *Metanoia* offered to those who were left in the path of a missed opportunity and the regret that accompanied it, *a chance to reflect and then transform.*

Metanoia, Greek meta-"after" and nous- "mind," is an afterthought or reflection of a missed opportunity, which can elicit a feeling of regret, but that can also result in a change or transformation in one's mind, in one's heart, in one's life. While there is an obvious element of regret inherent in *metanoia*, it does not come as a result of threats or shame or damnation. *Metanoia* comes from self-reflection and contemplation, and then from an awareness of God's lovingkindness, which results in *transformation.*[5]

The absolute beauty in this understanding of *metanoia* is that it gives a person the space to breathe and self-reflect and contemplate, to look inwardly and evaluate who they have become, to introspect and search their motives, their compulsions, their impulses, their heartaches, and their beliefs about others and themselves. It also gives a person room to breathe in the *shalom* of the Divine, to feel God's grace and acceptance, and take in the overwhelming love and kindness of God.

Yeah, I know. It is kind of mind-blowingly beautiful. It sounds so much different than the *repentance* we have been force fed. In *metanoia*, we do not hear the angry voices threatening us if we don't *repent*. Rather, we find space to look at ourselves honestly and begin the pathway to transformation.

LET THE TRANSFORMATION BEGIN

I love it when the forerunner of Jesus, John the Baptist, came on the scene wearing clothes made of camel hair while eating locusts and wild honey. I mean, if you are going to have some character prepare the way for Jesus, it has to be a wild-eyed chap wearing the mangiest camel hair clothing while eating bugs and honey, right? God bless that dude! And when wild-eyed John began his announcement, that called out like a voice in the wilderness, he proclaimed, "The *kingdom of God* has come near. Repent and believe the good news!"

What was wild-eyed John saying? Was he screaming and yelling at the people like an old time preacher pounding his fist and shaking his Bible? Was he yelling in a blood-curdling scream through a mic and speaker that people needed to repent or go to hell? Or, was he announcing something extraordinary and beautiful that was springing up and coming to life in the middle of the heartache, the pain, the suffering, and the wreckage of the world?

I believe it was the latter.

The *shalom* of God has always surrounded us. Each of us have been invited into this intimate, relational union with God and there is not one person who can keep you from it. And once you begin to see it, once you begin to taste it, you may stand in the wake of regret, contemplating and reflecting on all the ways you have missed God's forgiveness and lovingkindness in the past, but the profoundly good news is that the *shalom* of God is here with you and still inviting you in.

The Divine is telling you that you are loved. You are worthy. You are valued. And you have already been forgiven. So believe it. Live in light of it. Receive this beautiful invitation and then enter into it and be transformed by it! For the union of heaven and earth, the coming together of created and Creator has begun, even now in you. Taste and see just how good this life is!

It's a message, not of fear or eternal damnation, but of hope that this life can be better in the present, that it can be better in each of us. It is a good news message, not for select people, but for all people! And despite the wreckage that surrounds us. Despite the wreckage within us. Despite the wreckage we have created. Despite the wreckage to which we have contributed. The *shalom* of God is here and it is beginning to piece back together all of the broken pieces in wholeness, completeness, and harmony. And this transformation begins in you.

QUESTIONS

1. Has your understanding of *repentance* changed? If so, in what ways? If not, then why?

2. Why do you think that Jesus was so elusive in his parables? What are some insights you might gain from that?

3. What does contemplative space for self-reflection look like for you?

4. What does residing in *shalom* look like in the rhythm of your day? In the rhythm of your week?

5. How might the transformative experience of residing in *shalom* affect your mental health? Physical health? Emotional health? Relational health?

CHAPTER 8

Living as Presence

*All of humanity's problems stem from man's
inability to sit quietly in a room alone.*

BLAISE PASCAL

Music is all around us. All you have to do is listen.

AUGUST RUSH

Consider the lilies.

JESUS

It was our seventh day backpacking in the trail-less backcountry of Denali National Park in Alaska when we were
awakened by the early morning sunrise in Wolverine Creek. It
was going to be our biggest push yet- nine miles to exit- so we
needed an early start. The cloudless, blue skies welcomed our
early departure from camp.

The previous six days were the thoroughly definitive Alaskan
experience- bears, glaciers, bushwacking, territorial and aggres-
sive caribou, torrential rains, river crossings, and 40-degree late

summer temperatures. But even more, brilliant views, wild blueberries by the millions, mountain ranges too vast and too numerous to have even been named, and an absolute solitude devoid of any human activity, communication, noise pollution, or even a single, stray aircraft.

There was a sense of great satisfaction, deep refreshment, and imminent accomplishment even as we took our first steps forward that last morning.

Alaska could never be fully conquered, but it didn't conquer us.

And, we were about to finish something very few would ever have the honor and privilege of doing.

Grizzled and chiseled, we made our way through the gravelly and rocky Wolverine Creek toward Mt. Eielson. This rocky mount stands a mile above sea level and was our best and final hope of catching a glimpse of Alaska's crown jewel, Denali, which had eluded us for the previous six days.

Each labored step up the 60-degree sloped talus, which consisted of loose, softball-sized ankle busters, was aided by our trekking poles and closely accompanied by our heavy breathing. But ever so subtly, sneaking up on us westward, rising higher and higher with every foot of elevation gained, was the mighty, snow adorned Denali in all her glory.

Only seconds before, our breath was taken by strenuous activity and reduced oxygen level. But now, our collective breath was taken by sheer majesty.

As we reached the top of Eielson, no words were spoken, as if each of us already knew what to do and what the others were thinking.

There was a shared solemnity, a communal rite of the sacred and holy.

And along the ridge line we drifted apart, equidistant, to sit and stare and marvel and contemplate the beauty, to drink in the magnificence. It was an indescribably humbling, awe-inspiring, and deeply spiritual moment, quite certainly, the most spiritual experience of my life.

There was a familial union, an unbreakable bond between me, the creation, and the Creator. There birthed a moment of singularity between heaven and earth, of the two becoming miraculously one. The invitation was a present taste of that for which we have always so desperately longed, and have continued to expectantly anticipate, in all its fullness, at the consummation of the Ages.

My Lord, my God.

The truth is that we were always meant to be in *shalom* with the Creator and the creation.

We were always meant for wholeness, completeness, and harmony with all things.

And I was in that place, in that moment. It was so very good.

HUMAN DOINGS

But the forces of our present age are actually fracturing us into successive degrees of separation from this place of *shalom* and inhibiting us from experiencing this peace and abundance.

And it is evident in our busyness, in our technological attachments, in our detachment from real life, in our substance abuse and addictions, in our overconsumption, and in our utter obsession with the superficial to the neglect of our souls.

It is an understatement to say that our lives are full of an ever-increasing chaos that is choking and strangling the life out of us.

The culture we have created keeps us constantly seeking more and more stimulation, and we are never quite satisfied or at peace in stillness, let alone finding the essential refreshing of our souls in that space.

The culture in which we live and participate keeps us consuming and discarding, and we never quite find the satisfaction in what we have, let alone appreciate or find beauty in it.

We do not take the time to stop and realize how dependent and addicted we are to the noise and rush around us. Every single minute of the day is full of commotion and busyness. It is the television, music, conversations, kids, errands, to-do lists, and incessant chatter. When we finally come up for air we gasp, "God, where are you? This hardly feels like the abundant life you promised. Where is the peace?"

We don't stop to think how much our minds and bodies have become radically conditioned, dependent upon, and enslaved to the fast-paced motion of life and the constant, incessant stimulation.

And think about how this affects us.

We do not stop to listen to others. We are constantly thinking about what we are going to say next or do later or the next thing on our schedules. We are unable to concentrate and sit in silence and just listen and contemplate. We have to speak. We have to turn up the volume. We have to check our phones. We have to check social media and our messages and our emails. We bring our work home with us and never quite leave work. It just never stops. We just never stop.

It is no wonder we are so anxious, so impatient, so discontented, so addicted, and so over-medicated.

Our minds and bodies have become addicted and conditioned to this frenzied, hyper-stimulated rat race that has become our new normal.

We have been slowly evolving from a nature that exists and finds true life in *being* to an unnatural state of constantly *doing*. As others have accurately described, we have become less human *being*, and more human *doing*.

Where is the peace and contentment in that kind of life?

Where is the abundance that we were promised and for which we keep searching?

Where is this *life to the fullest* we long for and keep hoping to find one day?

This non-stop, daily grind culture that has blanketed us and ravaged us and devoured us makes it seemingly impossible to slow the pace and quiet those things around us and bring peace to our minds that feed on constant stimulation.

We are unable to just sit still and breathe, to contemplate, to find peace, to commune in the life-giving essence of God, and just be.

We are quickly becoming a people without a soul, a people pretending to be alive but who are dying from the inside-out. And this death is manifesting around us as we continue to neglect the ever-present invitation to life in the Spirit.

As Rohr accurately observed of our present condition, "We are a circumference people, with little access to our natural Center. We live on the boundaries of our own lives, 'in the widening gyre,' as [Yeats] puts it, confusing edges with essence, too quickly claiming the superficial as if it were substance. As Yeats predicted, things have fallen apart, 'the center cannot hold.'"[1]

We were created to be so much more than the lives for which we have settled. We were created to be so much more than the surface-level people who see the superficial as substance. We were created to

*be people of essence, people of the center, people who are fully awake
and fully alive and fully present each moment.*

SOLITUDE AND SILENCE

I sat down in front of the computer and put the first slide on
the screen. Plainly and directly it read, "Please take a seat
and remain quiet." Amidst the conversations and music on that
Sunday morning, and after seeing the instructions on the screen,
I heard someone say, "Yeah, good luck with that one." But as the
music faded and the conversations hushed to less than a whisper,
everyone slowly began to take their seats and the room became
completely silent.

The room settled into silence by a simple instruction on the
screen, but no one had any idea why they were being silenced.

Even more, they did not realize that we were going to sit
together in complete silence over the next forty-five minutes
while I taught using only words on the screen about the importance of solitude and silence. What began in discomfort and
unease by everyone in the room, ended in a new appreciation
of how much difference an hour of silence and contemplation
made in their souls.

*And I believe it took us experiencing it before we realized how
desperately we needed it. Not just in hour increments, even though
that is a great beginning point, but in our regular rhythm of life.*

In solitude and silence, we intentionally remove ourselves
from the noise, stimulation, busyness, distractions, chaos, and
the wreckage around us. We literally cut ourselves off from all we
have become addicted and dependent.

In solitude and silence, we metaphorically come out from where we have been hiding, behind the bushes and trees, to finally stand naked and exposed before God.

In solitude and silence, we are with God alone, as we experience the sweet embrace of heaven and earth unobstructed in this posture of receiving.

In solitude and silence we strip away all that has blanketed us and ravaged us and devoured us, leaving this now infinite void wide open and exposed, inviting the perfect freedom and perfect love, the *shalom* of God to come intimately close and to find residence within us.

This is the way our lives were always meant to be lived.

AN AWAKENING

It was an early fourth morning at Hance Creek, one of the few lush, vibrant ecosystems in the heart of the dry, arid, and unforgiving Grand Canyon. We had been on the trail-less Escalante Route the three previous days, hugging the mighty Colorado River in complete isolation, far from the usual touristy stops along the south rim and well beyond the maintained and frequented hiker trails that ascend and descend in and out of the canyon. We were in the rarely traveled backcountry of the Grand Canyon.

Our last ascent from Hance Creek would take us up a couple thousand feet to the visually stunning Horseshoe Mesa and then another thousand or so feet to our end destination at Grandview Point.

As we broke camp and steadily trekked toward the base of Horseshoe Mesa, there was a palpable and shared sense of excitement and trepidation. Excitement that we were conquering yet another highly-prized backpacking bucket list adventure that would add serious cred to our growing resume', but trepidation in knowing what kind of climb still stood between us and our exit.

The sun was already blazing in the near cloudless early morning sky and there was all but a single, lowly shade tree in front of us as we approached the towering mesa. We thought it would be the perfect spot for a quick drink and temporary reprieve from the sun before our big climb.

As we stood there in our short respite, one of the guys asked if I had any music on my phone. Usually I clear everything off of it in order to make room for all of the pictures I take during the trip, but to my surprise, there was one single song waiting in the queue.

And as I pressed play, we all quickly quieted.

In that one anticipatory moment, *Passing Afternoon* by Iron and Wine sweetly greeted us, and, to be honest, it felt as if I had never heard a song before.

There was an overwhelming intimacy I had never fully experienced through a song.

There was an acuteness to every sound, to every word sung. There was a simple, yet profound appreciation for every note, every melody, every harmony. There was a resonance in the depths of my soul that made this moment one of the most memorable of my life.

For four days the only sounds we heard were of nature- the blowing winds, the rushing waters, the melodious singing of birds, and each other's voices.

And in finding that space, it was nothing short of a peaceful and calm bliss that we each so desperately needed.

For the sounds of busyness and distraction had been silenced. Every tendency toward consumption had been vacated. An easing stillness cleansed and refreshed our souls.

And it was there where my appreciation was renewed.

I wasn't listening to a song as a means to distract, or as one trying to fill the void of an uncomfortable silence or as one simply consuming to consume, I was fully present and listening, as if for the first time, with deep appreciation.

Let me tell you.

There is something renewing and refreshing about purposefully removing oneself to find refuge in the stillness and quiet, or intentionally abstaining and then slowing reuniting. It is an essential discipline undertaken to be continually reminded of the resident goodness and simple beauty of all that we can all too easily take for granted.

And it is in this kind of intentionality, of seeking the refuge of stillness and quiet, of purposefully escaping the incessant activity, busyness, and noise of life, that moves us from a place of endless addiction, mindless consumption, and taking what we have for granted, to a place of simplicity and beauty, to a place of experiencing and appreciating all things anew.

I had this same kind of experience and depth of appreciation when I fasted for a week a few years ago. When I met with my brothers with whom I had been fasting over that week, we took the warm, homemade molasses and honey communion bread with a cup of deep, red earthy wine together to break our fast. There was an intensity and complexity in what I could smell and an explosion of diversity in what I could taste.

In that moment, I was thoroughly appreciative and truly thankful.

We were a few hundred feet from the highest point in the contiguous United States, Mt. Whitney. We had traversed

110-miles over eight arduous days through Kings Canyon and Sequoia National Parks, in areas too remote for even the strongest cellular signal.

It wasn't the first weeklong backpacking trip we had taken in which we were not able to communicate with our families. And it is always a surreal experience to be so remote, so off the grid that we have no way of hearing the voices of our loved ones, of knowing what is going on in the world, or knowing what kind of world we are walking back into.

But as we finally reached the 14,500 foot summit of Whitney, something unexpected happened. Our phones began to vibrate and ring continuously at different intervals, almost as if we were each receiving our own unique morse code messages, as they connected to service. As I looked down at the screen and began to read my text messages and then listen to my voicemails from my wife, my kids, and my mom and dad, tears began to stream down my face.

There was a sweetness and tenderness in their voices that I had too often overlooked or had not fully appreciated.

The truth is that we can very easily miss the simple beauty of those things that we take for granted, those things we quickly discard so we can consume more. And so much so, that we may not even appreciate the richness of what we have right in front of us, whether it be listening to a song, eating a meal, or enjoying the company of those we love.

For it's not in seeking more and more stimulation or consumption in which we find greater depths in this life. It is only in a regular rhythm of abstention, whether it be through solitude or silence or even fasting, where the Spirit can awaken our senses to discover and appreciate, moment by moment, all that we so easily take for granted.

This is the place where we once again find our hearts, even though it may feel like it is for the first time. This is the place where the thin veil between heaven and earth is pierced. This is the place of union and communion with the Divine. This is the sweet embrace of heaven and earth. This is our present eternal receiving. This is the place of resurrection and new life within. This is the place of presence and breathing in and breathing out *YHWH*.

This is *shalom*. This is where we begin to see and experience all things anew. Drink it all in.

INVITATION TO THE
SACRED AND HOLY

It doesn't take a mountain high in the backcountry of Alaska, a trek deep into the heart of the Grand Canyon, or an ascent to the heights of Mt. Whitney to discover this, for our eyes to be opened, for our hearts to come alive (even though escaping to the backcountry may certainly help).

All you have to do is walk outside and take a deep breath and accept the invitation.

Disconnect from all that enslaves you. Leave behind all that binds you and keeps you on the periphery and circumference of this life. Break free from your attachments and addictions. Turn off your phone, shut down your computer, power down your tablet, put them in the cabinet, go outside, and breathe in the Divine.

You are entering sacred and holy space.

Do you recognize it?

Do you see it?

Do you hear it?

Do you feel it?

Lie in the grass under a shade tree, feel the cool blades of grass beneath your fingers, let the wind blow over you. Meditate on the sounds of the birds and the swaying of the leaves on every branch of the tree. Consider every single detail of the rough bark on the tree and all of the busy insects moving hastily through every deep groove. Pick up a handful of dirt and just rub it between your hands and let it get underneath your fingernails. This is the goodness and mystery of life that immerses us.

Contemplate the Love and Beauty and Artistry within each thing. And how this Love surrounds you and how this Love holds you and how this Love invites you.

Spirit, Come!

Listen.

Smell.

Feel.

Close your eyes.

Take it all in and delight.

Let the wind blow at your back and let the sun shine down on your face. Listen to the conversations. Joy in the laughter of your children. Celebrate that you can give your baby a bath and change your baby's diaper. Delight in the songs of the birds and the rustling of the leaves. Be enveloped by everything and everyone around you.

Count your blessings.

Smell the autumn fragrance. Let the preparation of your meal be a prayer and a blessing. Savor every bite as if it is your very first. Feel the textures. Let the work of your hands be praise.

Count your blessings.

Enjoy friendship as you break bread at the table. Find life in mowing the lawn, washing the dishes, and in all the seemingly mundane. Be still and marvel at every star brilliantly shining in the night sky. Welcome both the sunshine and the rain. Rejoice in every good time and bad, for it is all worth it.

Count your blessings.

Sit in the woods and notice every detail of creation. Close your eyes and absorb every note and harmony. Glory in every drop of your morning coffee. Embrace the touch of another. Join in the chorus of all creation in praise.

Count your blessings.

It is good.

It is good.

It is good.

Is this humbling? Is this awe-inspiring? Is this miraculous? Is this deeply and profoundly spiritual? Is this Love embracing you and holding you and enveloping you? Is this love of the Creator calling your soul to greater breadths and depths? Is this love what your heart has always desired?

This is a taste of all we desperately long for in its fullness one day, but the goodness that we join in presently.

It is right here, right in front of us, waiting to be discovered and received. For those who seek it, will surely find it.

There is the ever-present reality into which we can reside, where love wholly embraces, where peace makes its home. It grows into a new way of living, a new way of seeing people and the world, and it becomes the perpetual outflow of our spirit.

And this reality is so much more than a singular event, so much more than a sporadic, momentary act, so much more than an expression of gratitude when the conditions are right. It is a an ever-flowing expression and heartbeat of presence and gratitude in everything, in every moment of the day, with every breath taken. And is never dependent upon the situations or circumstances of our lives.

From the depths of our souls and with every breath, we become this life-giving and ever-present reality.

We give thanks. It is so good.

The Psalmist writes, "You will go out in joy and be led forth in peace; the mountains and hills will burst into song before you, and all the trees of the field will clap their hands."[2]

QUESTIONS

1. Even though we were always meant for *shalom*, the age in which we live seems to work against that in so many ways, for example technology, busyness, commitments, etc. From your own experience, what are the biggest threats to *shalom* that you see in our culture? In your own life?

2. What is appealing to you in the disciplines of solitude and silence? What benefits might a person discover from the practices of solitude and silence?

3. In what ways are the disciplines of solitude and silence connected to *shalom*?

4. What would a realistic first step toward the disciplines of solitude and silence look like in your life?

5. How might the disciplines of solitude and silence affect how you begin to see or perceive or experience nature, music, conversations, relationships, time with loved ones, art, etc.?

CHAPTER 9

Community as Life

*When we try to pick out anything by itself, we find
it hitched to everything else in the Universe.*

JOHN MUIR

*And what am I supposed to do, but take good care, good care of
you? We have a lot of work to do, me and you, and you, and you.*

TONY DEKKER OF GREAT LAKES SWIMMERS

For as much intricate and detailed artistry that can be found in the most magnificent and individually unique trees that tower above the forest floor, there is an even more spectacularly confounding and revealing reality that exists underground, in the richness of the earth.

In all the ways that we may see a tree as this strong, rugged, and independent structure, the real beauty lies hidden from view below the earth's surface.

Within the larger forest, a single tree is not an isolated, self-reliant entity, but rather an essential, live-giving member of a larger, connected community that cares for the interest of the other.

Beneath the forest floor exists a vast fungal network of mycelium that connects the roots of the trees into an interdependent family that operates as a single, cooperative organism.[1]

These connections allow trees to pass essentials, such as nitrogen, carbon, phosphorus, and even water to each other. Astonishingly, these resources are shared by larger "mother trees" with other trees that may have a greater need. Even more, while these resources are preferentially shared by the "mother" with her offspring, there is no discriminating in the type of tree or plant that these resources are shared.

While there is a marvelous life, an individually unique and intricate beauty in what we observe in a single tree above ground, there is an even greater life and beauty in what connects them all together and in the life-giving, resilient, and cooperative community they share.

WE ARE CONNECTED

The same is absolutely true for us as well.

While our lives are individually unique and intricately beautiful in what we see in every single person, there is an even greater life and beauty in what connects and binds us together in the life-giving, resilient, and cooperative community we share with each other.

There is a union and communion with the Divine that gives each one of us life, that sustains us and holds us with every single prayerful breath we take, and that awakens and transforms us in a distinctly unique beauty.

But there is a holy Ground of Being into which we are each collectively rooted that does not leave us as isolated, self-reliant entities, but that thoroughly and inextricably joins us together as an integrated and interdependent, life-giving community that exists for the welfare of the whole.

While our soul's deepest longing is the present eternal receiving of *shalom* in our lives, the end destination of *shalom* is never with a single person. A single person is only the beginning point. *Shalom is only and always fully relational and communal.*

It moves and pulses and radiates outward from this new life we have discovered and received and then extends outwardly, binding us to others for the benefit of all, for the benefit of the larger cooperative community.

In the same way trees in a forest share essential nutrients and live-giving elements to each other through their deep connections, we too share in the life-giving elements of love and peace and grace that move out from our own individual lives of *shalom* to those with whom we are in intimate community, and then even further with others outside of our community.

The life-giving Spirit of God, which connects and binds us one to another, graces through our words, through our presence, through our deeds for the collective benefit of all, without discrimination.

HEALING RELATIONSHIPS

Of course there is an ideal that precedes the reality. What God intends for us is whole and healed relationships that exist in *shalom*. That is the goal, that each of us would find the wholeness and completeness and harmony of *shalom* in each of our lives and then extend that into each of our relationships.

And I know I am not surprising you when I say this, but this is incredibly difficult, because we will inevitably experience, or even cause, fractures in our relationships, whether they be with friends, spouses, family members, or other people with whom we come into contact throughout our lives.

We are not perfect. And I am certainly not perfect.

But I also have to balance all of that by saying that there are very few people guiding us into this ideal. The general narrative in most faith communities is to be a good person, to be a kind person, to be an upstanding citizen, but rarely, if ever, are we told to be those who work toward extending *shalom* in every interaction and every relationship, even though the majority of Jesus' teachings were relational.

It is enlightening, and kind of mind-blowing, that Jesus put a higher priority on us seeking *shalom* in our relationships than on our religious rituals and worship. In one of his teachings, he tells his audience that they should actually leave their gift at the altar if they remember that a brother or sister has something against them.[2] According to Jesus, forgiveness and restoration in the relationship is actually more important to God than our worship of God!

This is an absolutely radical teaching, if you think about it. Can you imagine telling church members that the doors of the building will be closed until each member reconciled with everyone who has something against them? No Eucharist. No worship songs. No Sunday School classes. No baptisms. Nothing. Leave your worship and go reconcile with your mom, your dad, your sister, your brother, your wife, your husband, and the guy at the grocery store whom you have wronged and then, and only then, can you proceed with worship. This is seriously radical stuff! But it gives you an idea of how essential it is for the *people of shalom* to be the *people of healing and restoration* above all else, even more than worshippers of God.

We are those whose roots extend deeply into this holy Ground of Being, who are being nourished in the *shalom* of the Divine, and then who begin to extend this nourishment to those around us- to every family member or friend we have hurt, to every person we have wounded, and to every enemy. These roots do not wait for hurt or wounded trees to cry out to us. These holy roots preemptively wrap around and seek to nourish our relationships with everyone around us, especially those we may have hurt.

So before we go any further, who have you hurt? Who have you wounded?

Are there relationships you have strained? Is there anyone with whom you need to reach out to right now and say that you are sorry? Is there anyone with whom you need to be reconciled? The posture of *shalom* in our lives is always humility. So go ahead, put this book down and meditate for a bit. Pray over your feelings and emotions and all of the people in your life. And then make that call or send that text. This is how *shalom* begins to move out for the healing of our relationships, for the healing of our communities, for the healing of the nations. It's possible that they may not want to reciprocate in the healing and mending in the relationship, but again, so long as it depends upon you... be peace.[3]

A NEW FAMILY

There is a deep, familial bond that exists among those who have been immersed and enveloped in the Divine, which takes our standard definition of family and turns it completely upside-down.

No longer is family defined by our genetics, but rather by our mutual union in the Spirit.

And I believe that is why Jesus asked, "Who is my mother, who are my brothers?"[4]

Clearly everyone knew who his mother and brother were (and Jesus knew as well), but Jesus challenged them to rethink the traditional family structure. He wanted them to see differently, to see more expansively, to see anew the beauty of what a family truly is and how this deeply rooted intimacy and care and cooperation extends beyond bloodlines.

For when we begin to understand that we exist in a broader kinship, that these deep roots are inextricably connected in this holy Ground of Being, we will begin to love and care for this larger family as a birth family should. And even more beautifully, this deeply rooted family will embrace and hold and nourish those who do not have, or who have never had, a birth family.

Shalom always moves beyond the single individual, in a deep and abiding love, for the benefit and care and nourishment of every individual and the larger family.

It is the way this life was always meant to be lived, and still can be. It is a family that cares so deeply for each other that they are willing to go to any length to demonstrate that love, even if it means their lives. And it is in this place where the shalom of God begins to extend far beyond ourselves.

The ancient words that were written by the Apostle Paul to the Colossian church echos this exact sentiment, "Let the *shalom* of Christ rule in your hearts, since as members of one body you were called to *shalom*."[5] As the *shalom* of God resides in each of us, it becomes that which we reside in together as we are intimately connected, as a body.

Again, *shalom* is only and always fully relational and communal. It can never exist in isolation. It was meant to exist in community, in a larger family.

ANOTHER DEVASTATION

I will never forget talking to Jeremy the day before his picture was to appear on the front page of our local newspaper. With his first words that evening, there was a sinking feeling in my body, from my upper chest to my lower intestines, and it felt like everything inside of me was endlessly falling. I have no idea what happens physiologically for this bizarre phenomenon to happen, but it is a helplessly nauseous sensation. It was a feeling I would carry with me throughout our brief conversation and then forward through the next year.

Jeremy, and his wife Jessica, have been our close friends for the last twelve years. We met them at the church we were attending at the time and it wasn't long before they joined us each week at our house church.

Jeremy worked at the local police department and after several years of successfully working patrol, in addition to being on the SWAT team, he moved into narcotics, where he would eventually take the lead as sergeant of narcotics. And being that this new position required irregular hours on a daily and weekly basis, we saw Jeremy less frequently on Monday nights when our house church gathered together.

I have to confess that when Jeremy called me that dreadful evening and told me he had resigned from his position with the police department for stealing drug evidence and then using the illegal drugs to satisfy his growing addiction to legally prescribed opioids, I couldn't help but to feel as if we had all failed Jeremy, failed Jessica, and failed their two elementary-aged boys.

This is a hard to say, but I think our roots were too shallow and our connection was weak at that time.

Certainly the distance Jeremy and his job put between us was a contributing factor, and maybe we trusted too much that Jeremy was doing fine on his own, but our roots should have been so much deeper, our connection in this Ground of Being should have been so much more pursuant and nourishing.

But we failed.

Our roots stayed close to home, stayed within our group, while our brother, the isolated tree, desperately needed nourishment.

It's possible to be in regular community with others and never develop strong, deep roots connected in the self-sacrificing, other-centered love of the Christ.

And that is the defining difference between groups of people that casually gather together, including many church groups, and the gathering of a community deeply rooted and grounded in the *shalom* of the Christ.

THE NEED FOR DEPTH AND INTIMACY

My wife and I have been in different church small groups over the last twenty years. We have developed some really good friendships and I am not diminishing them in the least, but at the end of the day, they were study groups. We got together, had some coffee and a dessert, and answered study questions with each other.

The relationships stayed largely at the surface and never went deeper. No one shared their individual or marital struggles.

No one shared what was really going on with their faith or the struggles and doubts they had. No one shared their deep pains, insecurities, or hardships.

In many ways, we were groups of people staying on the surface and going through the motions without ever developing anything deeper or more intimate. I am not blaming anyone for any of this. It is the nature of the product that we are putting out in our churches. It's just that it has to get deeper and more honest about who we are as individuals and what we are really dealing with and what we are really feeling and thinking and what we are really going through. It has to become less pretentious and less fearful and more real and more raw.

One only has to look at the trajectory of our culture to realize that people are starving for meaning, purpose, substance, real and intimate relationships, and a place to unpack all of the burdens they have been carrying around. This cultural trajectory affects every age demographic, but it is having the greatest impact on younger generations.

I met with a young man a while back who was addicted to heroin. He was involved in church leadership. He was actively involved and serving at his church in many capacities. All outward signs look good, but yet he was silently wrestling with the demons of addiction. When this was discovered by the other church leadership, and after he went through drug rehab successfully, he was told not to discuss it with anyone in the church, so he carried this brokenness with him in isolation, while the church maintained the image of being good and whole and perfect.

It is examples like this, and I have witnessed many over the years, that continue to prove to me that faith communities of the future will be those that gather together more intimately, and less formally, to talk about our faith, to share our hearts and our stories, to honestly discuss our heartaches, burdens, and struggles, and to give examples of how God is working in each of our lives. It may look ugly at times. It may be utterly heartbreaking at times. It may even begin to change people's perceptions that the church is actually made up of imperfect people.

But that is what we desperately need right now. We do not need communities of perfection. We need communities of brokenness that are deeply rooted in the Ground of Being and that carry and sustain one another in this deep and abiding love.

Faith communities of the future must be an equal playing field. And everyone, no matter who we are, whether it be a pastor, an elder, a lay-people, or simply a seeker, must realize that we are all in the same place before God, that we all need to bare our hearts and souls to one another without fear, and that we all need the encouraging words, love, prayers, and care of the others.

Faith communities of the future will be raw and bare bones in its vulnerability and honesty, and also renown for its depth and hunger for the Christ. They will be faith communities that lack pretense, judgment, and self-righteousness and simply invites people to come together around a table, to roll up their sleeves, and to speak with an honest hearts in pursuit of the healing and restoration of God, even when there are a few F-bombs or when we are joined by someone who is drunk or high.

The table of the Christ always has room and there is always an empty seat of invitation for everyone.

It's only in this non-sterile, unvarnished, and truth-seeking place of meeting where the sick, all of us, can meet together with the doctor. It's only in this place where the doors of our hearts will be unlocked, and where the dark places that we have so easily hidden from each other will finally be opened and exposed to the light.

Faith communities of the future will be around tables- breaking bread and taking the cup together. And it is in this place where we move from a personal, individualized faith to a place of shared, relational, and communal faith as a family, a community with deep and intimately connected, nourishing roots.

And this kind of shared and relational community, that is deeply rooted in the Christ, is always and unequivocally defined by a love in which one would go to any and every length to embody and express the love and peace of God to others.

And it is a love and peace that is deeply rooted and always extending outward, working toward the nourishing and sustaining of another. It is a community that does not simply exist in a confined, isolated, individualized space of *shalom*, but that moves outwardly to invite others into that sacred space as well, to invite others to the table of invitation.

WE GREW DEEPER

But up to the point of Jeremy's resignation, we were a group of friends who got together and did a Bible study. His resignation and then his time in drug rehab, finally showed us how shallow our roots had been and how this had contributed to our friend withering in isolation without the nourishment of our family.

I am sorry Jeremy, Jess, Max, and Owen.

We should have done so much more.

We just should have done so. much. more.

It wasn't even thirty minutes after our conversation had ended on the phone that evening when Jeremy's face was being plastered and shared all across social media. I knew how utterly devastating this was for me, so I could not even begin to imagine how devastating it was for Jeremy and Jess, and then for their boys, who would have to go back to school the next day and face their classmates.

Jeremy is an unbelievably great guy who, in the throes of addiction, made terrible decisions and was now going to pay the price for it, not just in the court of public opinion, but more importantly, in a court, standing before a judge, where he would eventually be facing multiple felonies and misdemeanors.

During the time Jeremy was in rehab, and before his impending arrest, our roots began to grow quickly as we surrounded Jess and the boys. We held them and supported them in ways that had previously been foreign to us. We made meals for months. We did handyman jobs around their house. We helped with picking up the kids and watching them. We discreetly helped with finances. We held them in their tears. We embraced them. We prayed over them.

There were so many unknowns about the future and what it would look like for them, for us, but in the present moment, we grew more closely, we grew more deeply, than we ever had been.

But it didn't end there. When Jeremy came home from rehab, the roots of our deep and growing love surrounded him and held him as well. These were the months of unknowing. These were the months when we were being suspended and held up through our deep and abiding love. These were the months of waiting for the police investigation to end and the arrest to be made.

And then, there was the shocking announcement.

Unpredictably, unimaginably, Jeremy and Jess told us they were expecting a baby, right in the middle of the police investigation.

I know.

I had the same reaction. It was a reaction of profound joy and excitement, but also a reaction of dumbfounded fear. What if

Jeremy goes to prison for years? What if Jessica has to be a single mom raising three young kids by herself? Would we be able to get through this together? And if so, how would we do it? What would that even look like?

With each question, we drew closer. We were no longer isolated, self-reliant trees. We were a deeply rooted, intimately connected, nourishing and sustaining forest of a family. We would be able to do this, because there was a Spirit binding us together in shalom. We were in this thing, united as one.

To be honest, it is what we should have always been, but what we ultimately became, and what we had to absolutely be for each other, as the following weeks and months led to Jeremy's arrest and sentencing to jail time, which was then quickly followed by Abbott's accident and death just a couple of months later. These were the times that we needed each other more deeply than we could even imagine.

What we learned, and even more, what we have become together, is something so indescribably beautiful. It is something that has grown up and blossomed right in the middle of all our pain and suffering, right in the middle of the wreckage and devastation that surrounds us. There is a holy and divine connection, a deeply abiding love that knits us and holds us together, and it is this kind of community that must extend outward.

EVERYONE NEEDS THIS FAMILY

Amid the wreckage of a world with parents who have lost a child or children, children who have lost parents, broken families, orphaned and abandoned children, widows and widowers, and those who have been alienated by their birth families, there is unparalleled life and beauty to be found in this deeply rooted, intimately connected family that is united and held together in the Christ.

Amid the wreckage of a culture with social outcasts, homeless individuals with nowhere to go, men and women locked behind bars, the disabled who have been abandoned, and the person stigmatized and judged by society, there is unparalleled life and beauty to be found in this deeply rooted, intimately connected family that is united and held together in the Christ.

This is the family in which all are always welcomed and loved and held and sustained. It is a family that knows no outcast, no stranger, no alien. For all are welcomed into this community and all have a seat at the table.

And it is in this family that, when we all gather together and sit around the table, we know that no matter the forces that have come against us, and no matter how much we each have been torn to pieces throughout the day, the love of God brings us back together and, through this family, nourishes us and sustains us and carries us. And together, we can courageously face another day, another week, another year because we have a family ready to embrace us and shower us with love and support and encouragement and acceptance.

What an unbelievably beautiful family.

STORIES, TEARS, AND EMBRACES

While Jeremy was in jail and just before Abbott died, our house church finished a thirteen-week study on the letter of 1st Corinthians. And as we talked through the last question, which asked which part of the study had challenged us the most through the thirteen studies, we realized we had been doing the study for significantly longer than thirteen weeks. In fact, we had been doing the study for so long that we had to flip through the study book to remember some of the content and highlights.

But in a somewhat comical twist, our flipping through the study books became less about finding and remembering the highlights than trying to figure out when we actually started the study.

And it didn't take long before someone finally located the date when we asked the first question in the first lesson.

We started the study in October 2015. It was now February 2017.

I'm no mathematician, but that's a little more than thirteen weeks. It's something closer to seventy weeks!

We were blown away and had a really good laugh about it.

It's probably no surprise to you, after reading most of this book, that I have a way of taking any spontaneous occasion of hilarity or incredibly mundane moment and making it a serious and poignant life lesson. I say that somewhat tongue-in-cheek, but the truth is that I always try to make any moment profoundly spiritual.

And that was what I was about to do on that Monday night after realizing we had been doing a thirteen week study for seventy weeks.

As I have already mentioned, I have led and been a part of a dozen or so house churches, or small groups, over the last twenty years. Even more, I have headed up Small Group Ministries in churches for close to a decade, writing curriculum, training group leaders, and helping people find groups in which to connect. I have done it all with small groups.

But if there is any mistake I have made in the past, and believe me there are way too many to count, it is that I treated these small, intimate gatherings as a theoretical model to be implemented, or a mechanical process to control and make predictable and uniform, rather than seeing them a part of a vibrant, life-giving forest where lives and relationships, like trees, are deeply rooted and connected, nurtured and sustained, in the deep and abiding love of Christ.

The truth is that it is all too easy for each of us to live in isolation and to remain undetected below the radar, without ever having to invest in deeper-than-the-surface relationships or in the complexities of other people's lives.

The truth is that it is all too easy to for each of us to make excuses as to why we don't want to get involved in community with people we may not *completely* agree with, without ever having another pour out their heart and soul to you, without ever having to walk through life's messiness together, without ever having to lean on others when life seems too overwhelming.

The truth is that it is all too easy for each of us to live each day simply checking items off our to-do lists, while remaining a nameless, faceless body, without ever having to carry another person's burdens, without ever having to pray over their utter brokenness, or without ever having to give someone words of encouragement, blessing, healing, and life.

In my experience, the only place where the superficial veneer is stripped away, where pretense is obliterated, where cosmetic application fails, and where vulnerability is unmasked and triumphantly exposed is in the deeply rooted, Divinely-connected presence of an unconditionally loving, non-judgmental, other-centered group of trusted friends.

That is the very essence, the very heartbeat of community.

That is what I learned and shared that night with my closest friends in my house church.

There is something that happens between the study questions that is deep and profound and impossible to quantify.

And that's exactly why our study took seventy weeks, rather than thirteen.

Because between the questions,

There were stories.

There were tears.

There were laughs and smiles.

There were embraces.

There were celebrations.

There was real life happening- in all of it's unrehearsed, unglamorous grit and raw emotion.

Between the questions were strained marriages.

There were friends, family members, and pets passing away.

There were the challenges of parenting.

There were jobs that had been lost or changed.

And there were our personal failures.

Between the questions were doubts, hopelessness, and shattered hearts.

But even more, between the questions, there was the goodness and grace of God embodied. There was an undying love and care for one another. There were tearful embraces. There were uplifting words of encouragement. There were prayers of healing and blessing. There were so, so, so many moments of celebration. And all of this, always, with an open door and open arms.

We were so much more than a "church group' trying to complete a thirteen-week study or trying to find the right answers to Bible study questions.

It was more incarnational than mental.

It was more shared experience than class work.

It was more living out the answer than finding it.

That's what brought me to tears.

That's what made me so incredibly thankful for my friends with whom I get to share my life.

It was truly the essence of a deeply rooted, life-giving of community.

And it is into this Ground of Being which every, single person in the world was meant to be rooted and intimately connected, as well.

A TRUE SEEKER

The rain intensified as we stared out the large windows into the darkness and talked about our next backpacking trip. We were killing a few moments while waiting for one more guy to show up to our weekly confession gathering.

It is worth noting at the outset that our gatherings are never without incident.

The building in which we meet is nestled quite conveniently in a downtown residential area where substance abuse, domestic violence, and crime is commonplace. We have rushed outside on various occasions to play peacemaker by breaking up fights, praying with those who are high or drunk, giving food to those who are hungry, offering shelter to those who are homeless, and comforting those who have been abused. While we show up weekly for our own benefit, there is no doubt that we are really there for the people of the neighborhood.

And on this particular rainy night, it would be no different.

The door opened and a thoroughly soaked young man, about 20-years old, walked in and threw himself down on one of the vacant 1980's sofa chairs, as if we had been expecting him. And by our response to him, he may have thought that we were indeed expecting him, as we greeted him with the delight of a long, lost friend.

"I'm drunk," he stated, almost expecting us to be horrified.

We didn't take the bait.

A drunk guy walking into a church building seemed like the best dry place to be at that moment. Plus, we had all rattled the bottle at some point in our lives, so we were no different than our wet acquaintance.

"What's going on man? Just wanting to get in out of the rain?"

Reaching for a sober thought he said, "I walk by this place all the time and wanted to come in to see what's going on. I guess the alcohol gave me the courage this time."

We were certainly glad he did and told him as much. Whether the conversation was vodka-induced or not, it really didn't matter. This guy was clearly seeking something. And we were privileged to be the ones who could potentially help him find it. We just didn't know how desperate he was to find it.

"I've been thinking about killing myself lately."

"Oh yeah, why have you been thinking that," we asked gently.

"Because I don't have a purpose in life. I think about it all the time and I have come to the conclusion that since I have no purpose, there is no reason to live."

He continued with his line of thinking.

"My friend told me that if God wants us to be at peace, and if death will give me peace, then God wants me to die so I will be at peace. So I have thought about killing myself."

All I could feel at that moment was a deep and profound sense of sadness. Yes, for him, but even more so for the millions and millions of people in our country who are just as confused and hopeless, without a deeply-rooted, intimate community in which they are held and sustained and loved.

There is a very real dichotomy between the elegant and beautiful movements of *shalom* that grows out of deeply rooted, intimate, welcoming, cooperative community and the superficial, depersonalized, and divisive spirit of our culture.

And one only has to look at the wreckage around us to realize that people are completely exhausted with all of the antagonism and finger-pointing and division.

People of all ages, very much like this young man, are atrophying and dying in isolation and desperately need life-giving, life-sustaining relationships and community that is deeply-rooted and cooperative, that has purpose and substance and a place to unpack all of their burdens and heartache they have been carrying around.

And it is my belief that this tension is leaving a growing number of people questioning their worth, their value, and their purpose in life.

The truth is that we each have a longing to know that our lives matter, that there is a purpose for which we live, and that there is a community in which we are an essential and integral part.

And on that rainy night, we were witnesses to both the wreckage and the longing. The cry amidst the scattered parts was for someone, anyone to help make sense of the devastation. From that vantage point, all one can see is rock bottom. All one can feel is utter hopelessness.

Who can help me in this place of hopelessness?

Who can save me from this isolation I am experiencing?

Who can help me make sense of my life that is falling apart?

Is there not a community where I can find my life again?

He was asking the right questions, at the right time, to the right people.

But, too many times, I wonder if those in the same exact situation as this young man are left completely alone in their brokenness, questioning their worth, value, and purpose in this life, and standing in their own personal wreckage with unanswered questions.

As those who have been in the wreckage ourselves, and as those who have searched for our own identity and purpose in the devastation, we should be those who have not just discovered the beauty of deeply rooted and intimately connected community, but those whose roots now extend outward for the care of others.

"I don't think that God wants you to die. In fact, God wants you to live, and to live a full life. And I am not quite sure that a full life and peace is found in death."

I had his complete attention.

"There are two ways," I started.

"One way is full of life, love, joy, kindness, unity, peace, turning the other cheek, forgiveness, mercy, service, grace, and hope...and it is beautiful and our hearts long to be a part of something so exquisite. That is the deep and abiding way of the Christ. That is where we find our true identity and our true purpose in this life. We are deeply rooted and connected to one another in the Christ. And that is what you are being invited into right now."

I could see his eyes beginning to tear up as if he had never imagined that such a life was possible. The roots were extending outward.

And then I continued.

"But there is also another way. There is the way of death, hatred, bitterness, revenge, retaliation, division, self-centeredness, rage, resentment, judgment, pride, and despair. This way is not the *shalom* we find in God. And it is this kind of existence that strips away our true identity, our true purpose in this life, and our nourishment in this ground of being."

"I don't want that," he said.

We all stood together, embraced as brothers, and began to pray. And it felt as if the prodigal son had come home. Home to the open arms of the Father through the embrace of a few guys who realized that we are all deeply rooted and intimately connected to the Source of all Life and to each other in this ground of being.

It was a beautiful moment in the wreckage and devastation that night, and what the future of a deeply rooted and intimately connected community looks like in an increasingly divided and hostile world.

And it is in this place where we move from a individualized, isolated faith to a place of shared, relational, and communal faith as a family.

That is the beauty of the deeply rooted and intimately connected, community of the Christ that exists in an other-centered love that nourishes and sustains. And it is in this type of community where the table always has room and there is always an empty seat of invitation for everyone.

QUESTIONS

1. When you think about a life-giving, resilient, and cooperative community, what does that look like in real life? Share a time when you have either experienced, or been a part of, that type of community. If you haven't, why do you think that type of community is so hard to find?

2. What obstacles keep people from developing deeply-rooted, intimately connected relationships and community?

3. List some reasons why this type of integrated and interdependent, life-giving community is beneficial for those who are connected to it?

4. How might this type of community be beneficial for neighborhoods, cities, and countries?

5. Why do you think *shalom* can only truly flourish and be realized in relationships and community?

CHAPTER 10

When Shalom Goes Forth

Love and faithfulness meet together,
righteousness and shalom kiss each other.
Faithfulness springs forth from the earth,
and righteousness looks down from heaven.

THE PSALMIST

There is an ancient cave dwelling where people have been imprisoned since birth. Their feet and necks have been chained in a fixed position so they can do nothing but look straight forward, day after day, at the cave wall in front of them. Adding to the intrigue and mystery of this strange living condition, immediately behind the prisoners, is a constructed wall with a fire that burns brightly behind it.

Each day people enter the cave and stand behind the constructed wall, holding up puppets that look like animals and people, both rising high above the wall. The shadows of the puppets dance along the cave wall for the prisoners to see and interpret. The noises they hear, they believe, come from the shadows. They do not realize that the shadows are simply projections of puppets being held up in front of a fire, nor do they realize that there are real people inside the cave holding up the puppets.

This is the only reality they have ever known.

One day a single prisoner was freed from his shackles and began to look around the cave. He noticed the wall immediately behind him and the fire that was blazing even farther back in the cave. He was told that what he is seeing is reality and that what he had been experiencing all of those years in shackles was a very limited reality. Upon receiving this shocking and difficult to comprehend information, and in addition to the fact that his eyes were hurting from the bright light of the fire, in his pain and fear, he ran back to the chains. The only life he ever knew.

But before he was able to put back on the chains, he was dragged away from his comfortable, limited, and shackled existence, and up a steep ascent that led passed the wall and passed the fire to the opening of the cave.

Outside of the cave was a magnificently blue sky with large puffy, white cumulus clouds hanging suspended around the warm, radiant, yellow sun. There were miles of rolling, lush, green grass. It was nothing like he had ever seen. But this entire experience, of being dragged up the stairs and into the blinding light of the sun, was extraordinarily painful for the prisoner and it made him very angry.

As the moments passed, however, the now free man eventually calmed down, his eyes adjusted to the bright light, and he began to observe a depth of reality and a spectrum of color that he could have never imagined in his previous existence. He saw the blue sky, the white clouds, the green grass, the sunset. He saw stars begin to dot the black night sky and the luminescence of the full moon. He even saw crowds of people gathering around, each of them with so much more detail and definition in their appearance than the human-shaped shadows that he used to watch every day in his chains.

He realized very quickly that he preferred this new, expansive, vibrant reality to his previous reality in the cave looking at shadows each day. And it was at that point when he thought of his fellow prisoners in the cave, still chained in their dimly lit existence, and how desperately he wanted them to experience this new life-giving reality that he had discovered.

So he went back inside to release them from their chains.

FROM THE CHAINS, A NEW REALITY

Of course this is an absurd, highly improbable allegory. And I am sure that you are relieved to know that this isn't a real situation happening in some remote corner of the world by a group of highly unethical researchers!

But seriously, this paraphrased short story was inspired by a writing entitled *Allegory of the Cave,* which is one of the most famous writings of Plato from his 4th century BC work *Republic.*[1]

In the cave story, Plato used symbols and metaphors to describe the present condition of humanity in the world. He surmised that it is all too easy to be locked and shackled into an existence we have only known from birth, and then to only know and experience this limited reality, in which we mistake shadows, echoes, and chains for real life.

Even more, Plato detailed movements away from these chains and toward the light of a new reality and how this new reality may initially invoke fear and lead to experiencing pain before enlightenment, before seeing all things anew.

I share this story, not in any way insinuating that you are the one in chains who needs dragged out of the cave kicking and screaming to see this new and beautiful reality, even though that may very well be true for you. You may be experiencing your own personal cave, where you have been living contained and shackled day after day within the walls where shadows are mistaken for real life.

You may have been there as long as you can remember and are just now coming to the realization that you have been chained to tradition, expectations, religion, or the everyday grind of life for too long. You may have arrived in that place while deconstructing everything you thought you knew about faith, religion, or spirituality and have been shackled without any apparent place to go from there. You may have been in the cave without ever realizing that the chains have already been removed and that there is an opening that is awaiting you, into a more expansive, more beautiful, and more life-giving way of living than life in the cave.

Only you can be the judge of that for yourself.

Rather, I share this story to turn the prism of perspective just slightly so that we may appreciate yet another angle of beauty.

When someone discovers and experiences a new, different, and more beautiful reality, they want others to experience it as well. However, it is impossible for someone to extend that which they have not first experienced for themselves. And when a person mistakes shadows and chains for real life, that is the only reality they live within and then the only reality they can share with others.

This is where we find ourselves today in our culture.

WHAT WE BECOME

As we have neglected to understand our fundamental and essential need for *shalom* as the source and center of our lives and of our communities, we have acquiesced to darkness and shadows. We have neglected justice and have ignored righteousness. We have walked blindly along crooked paths. We have stumbled along and groped the walls like people who do not have the eyes to see.

> The way of [*shalom*] they do not know;
>> there is no justice in their paths.
> They have turned them into crooked roads;
>> no one who walks along them will know [*shalom*].
> So justice is far from us,
>> and righteousness does not reach us.
> We look for light, but all is darkness;
>> for brightness, but we walk in deep shadows.

Isaiah 59: 8-9

We essentially exist as actors in which the only script we have been given, the only script we know, is one that lives out of our disconnection from the Divine and the brokenness that is the result of our disconnection. And to be honest, that appears to be the script from which everyone is reading and taking their cues these days. As we have believed that this single script is what dictates our character, governs how we relate to the other characters, and informs how we exist within the plot of this real life drama, we have, in reality, become something so far from what we were ever intended to be.

Our ignorance of shalom frustrates justice and inhibits righteousness.

But how does one invite others to take part in a better script when this is the only script we have ever been given, when this is the only script from which we have ever read, when this is the only script we have ever known? As this is the only source material from which we have read, it becomes the only source that informs our roles, and we act accordingly.

It is essentially the old saying, "You are what you eat."

Or, to sound more erudite, "What you feast upon, you become."

Or, to sound more parental, "You are the company you keep."

Or, to sound more spiritual, "What you worship, you become."

Or, to quote a guy from Celebrate Recovery, "If you keep going to the barber you're going to get a haircut."

Any life principle that can be arranged into that many applicable variations, must have an essential truth at its center.

When we make our source the very brokenness that surrounds us, we invite it to be our emotional center which begins to ravage our spiritual and physical well-being, which then begins to manifest outwardly in our lives, further inflaming the rapidly intensifying fires of hostility that we face every day and further fanning the flames of injustice and unrighteousness.

Anger only breeds more anger.

Hatred only leads to more hatred.

Division only builds more walls and creates more divisions.

Retribution only cycles into more retribution.

Violence only escalates into more violence.

It is the same tired, eye-for-an-eye, tit-for-tat game that has been played for all of human history, and it is still the greatest of our individual and societal ills. We feed upon the carnage that we face, which only further impoverishes us.

And as we have starved and neglected our soul, we are close to losing it, individually and collectively.

Rather than fully drinking in the *shalom* of God, this union and communion with the Divine, it is way too easy to begin feasting upon brokenness and anger and rage and fear and hatred, which are always readily available for our consumption. And, it becomes the negative energy by which we begin to live.

There is absolutely nothing unique or beautiful or life-giving in becoming the very ugliness and hostility and death that we face. And there is absolutely nothing in this negative energy that will remedy the deep, soul-level issues and wreckage we carry within us and that surrounds us.

LIVING IN FEAR

Even as I write these words, there is an epidemic of fear spreading among many in our country, including Christians. There are the fears of terrorism, illegal immigrants, presidents, differing ideologies, global instability, and just general xenophobia. And it is absolutely essential that we confront this culture of fear. So to all reasonable (and even all unreasonable) people, especially Christians, let me say that *fear is absolutely not of God and fear has absolutely no place in the life of one who follows Jesus.*

The Scriptures say that, "There is no fear in love. Complete and perfect love turns fear out the doors and expels every trace of terror!"[2]

So when we are completely and perfectly consumed in the *shalom* of God, fear vanquishes and has no hold or grip on our lives, because it has been replaced by the love of the Divine.

And being a people consumed by love, rather than fear, matters.

Because as the world becomes even more chaotic and is turned completely upside-down, those who are stricken in fear will see the fearless example of those who have been consumed by the complete and perfect love of the Divine, who have been immersed in the *shalom* of God, and they will long it for as well.

For this love that flows from a life of *shalom* will never fear.

It is not afraid of governments.

It is not afraid of politicians or their laws.

It is not afraid of economic turmoil or collapse.

It is not afraid of illegal immigrants.

It is not afraid of any refugee from any part of the world.

It is not afraid of threats or scare tactics.

And it certainly is not afraid of one single terrorist.

Listen.

Governments will make decisions based on their own interests. The media will sell a message even if it is misleading or is propaganda. Enemies will threaten violence from here to eternity. But as people of *shalom*, we will never fear. No matter the situation or circumstance. Our only response is love.

For fear has no lasting residence within us. It is only the complete and perfect love of God that remains.

And this love is an immense ocean that swallows whole the tiniest speck of sand that is fear and death.

This love is a universe that consumes and overwhelms the microscopic atom of fear and death.

This love is the Alpha and Omega, the Beginning and End that conquered fear and death once and for all at the cross of Calvary and proved it on Resurrection morning.

And this love transcends all things- politics, nationalities, groups, sects, tribes, tongues, races, sexual orientation, and any other construct that works to divide us.

This love transcends religion, denominationalism, doctrines, theological opinions, and everything else about religion that oppresses and works to divide people.

This love transcends our every issue, our every conflict, our every division, and answers sufficiently our every question and how we should respond to every situation and to every person.

And when you have experienced a love that immense, that overwhelming, you can do nothing but let it wash over you. You can do nothing but share that love with everyone. You have been changed at the very depths of your soul forever. And you so badly want to share that love with others that you would be willing to go to any length, even giving up your own life, for others to experience the complete and perfect love of God.

That is how a culture of fear is obliterated, by the love of God.

DESPERATE FOR AN ALTERNATIVE

And this is the alternative that we need for the vicious cultural cycles to end. We need a growing movement of dreamers and revolutionaries and prophets from community to community who envision a different way of seeing and an alternative way of living in the world.

We need a people rising in the radical resurrection of *shalom*, who have flipped the script, and who will take this great light into the darkness, who will straighten these crooked paths, who will be repairers and restorers of this great breach of injustice and unrighteousness, and who will stand up, even in the face of intimidation, violence, and impending death, to be the resurgence of love and beauty in the wreckage.

Resistance is not enough. We must become shalom. And then we must take this shalom courageously with us, as we revolt against this present darkness together.

There is absolutely nothing more beautiful and revolutionary than when the unsurpassable peace and love of God's *shalom* pours into each of us, becoming our collective center, becoming our collective source, and then that which we begin to carry with us, as we lock arms in community, as a family, and carry this light of peace and love into the world.

This is how the cycle will ultimately end.

This is how these dead bones will begin to rise.

This is how love will decisively win.

This is how beauty will flourish in the wreckage.

The reality is that there is not a single one of us who can face the Everest of issues, problems, conflicts, antagonisms, and hatreds of this broken world and then begin to share *shalom*, without *shalom* first becoming our center, without *shalom* first becoming the source by which we live our lives.

And one must first be *shalom* to stand up to and drive out the grievous inhumanity of our time with the unparalleled and other-worldly *shalom* of the Divine.

It is this exact principle by which Martin Luther King Jr., not only spoke and preached, but also lived out and demonstrated in the face of the terrible, hostile, oppressive, and dehumanizing forces of hatred and evil. In his courageous wisdom and amazing love he reminded the world that, "Returning hate for hate multiplies hate, adding deeper darkness to a night already devoid of stars. Darkness cannot drive out darkness; only light can do that. Hate cannot drive out hate; only love can do that."[3]

And I am confident this was exactly what Jesus was referencing when he told his disciples that he has *food to eat that they know nothing about.*[4] Only the holy center and holy source of *shalom* can bless those who curse, can repay evil with good, and can love an enemy.

Even more, Jesus said, "*Shalom* I leave with you; my *shalom* I give you."[5] And it is this *shalom* that we have been given by the Christ that we are to carry with us into this present darkness. *Shalom* is our wellspring of wholeness and completeness and harmony in all things into which we have been freely invited to receive with open hands. It is the only food that can sustain us and help us grow and produce fruit. It is this intimate union and communion of life in the Divine that is our absolute Source of nourishment.

In *shalom*, we find our unique food and absolute nourishment that doesn't just barely sustain us as we limp along through life, but that actually gives us an incomprehensible peace and love and joy and freedom that does not shrink or fade away in the face of inconveniences, trials, tribulations, injustices, or even death. And it is this wholeness, completeness, harmony, and oneness with the Father from which grace and peace and love explode through our lives and revolt against the dark, hostile, divided, and oppressive forces of this world.

LIFE MATTERS NOW

Many of you are likely wondering why you have never heard anything like this in your churches. Or, why you have never heard anyone in your church talk about *shalom*. Or, why your preachers or pastors have never preached about you becoming *shalom* and then taking this *shalom* as a revolution against this present darkness of this world.

The truth is that our churches have completely missed the big picture.

And while it would be easy to critique all of the ways that churches are misaligned, and believe me there are many, I want to focus on the one belief that has been the most counter-productive to our lives, relationships, communities, and creation. It is the belief of a spiritual heaven where saved people will go for eternity, as the earth is ultimately destroyed. It is the preaching of how terrible the world is and how desperately we need Jesus to save us and help us escape this world so that we can go to heaven one day.

But that was never the message of Jesus, not is it the point of this faith.

We have unfortunately maintained a mindset that is largely disconnected from, and devoid of, the present. It is a mindset that sees darkness as a present inevitability from which we all need to escape. It is a mindset that believes the point of life is to be a "good person" until Jesus comes to take us all away to eternity in heaven. It is a mindset that is content simply waiting around for a spiritual heaven so that we can escape this terrible world, while our present darkness grows even darker and our paths grow even more crooked, for the way of *shalom* we have neglected.

Meanwhile, justice continues to abandon us and righteousness remains far from us.

The truth is that we begin living presently in light of the future we envision, for better or worse.

If a person is only focused on getting to a future spiritual heaven, they will begin doing things presently to make sure they have "security" to "get to heaven one day." And then, they will spend time thinking of ways to "get others to heaven," as well. That is why there is such an obsession with saying the right words, following the correct steps, and then trying to convert people. It is all about getting to heaven and getting as many people as possible to this future heaven.

And to that end, Jesus has become nothing more than a ticket to get to heaven, rather than the way to an abundant and full life of shalom presently.

It reminds me of the age old debate that many have about whether or not a person will "go to heaven" if they die on the way to their baptism.

Faith has been so tragically reduced and watered down to simply making a decision exclusively for the purpose of "making it to heaven," that people have no knowledge that *faith is for the purpose of the present.*

That is why a significant majority of the American Church, to a great extent, is indifferent to the present, real world efforts of peacemaking, reconciliation, restorative justice, creation care, and standing on the side of, and becoming a voice for, the marginalized, oppressed, victimized, stigmatized, and those pushed to the edges of society.

Because when one's beliefs are only focused on making a single decision to "trust in Jesus" in order to escape the wreckage of this life, rather than embracing the beauty and wonder and grace of this abundant life all around us, and then presently becoming the *shalom* that we hope for and anticipate in our future, we have completely and monumentally missed the point.

When it is *shalom* that we do not know, it is no surprise that we continue in this present darkness with labels and divisions and dividing lines.

It's no wonder that we continue to perpetuate a fragmented and broken reality of hierarchies and belonging-systems that exist in hostility and conflict with each other.

It's no wonder that we have become so tightly fused with politicians and the political parties and their divisive games.

It's no wonder we have been immersed in nationalism and taken on the characteristics, attributes, and values of our country.

It's no wonder that we continue to play the religious games of who can have a seat at the table of invitation and who can't.

It's no wonder that our prayers are for God to rescue us from this evil, hostile, and divided world.

We have significantly contributed to the very problems we are trying to escape.

And to be honest, that is the reason why many have abandoned, and are continuing to abandon, the American Church.

They view it as irrelevant to their lives because it is indifferent to the great cultural and social issues we face.

And all I can say is that I don't blame them.

LET IT BEGIN NOW

But if there is any good news at all, it is that there is actually a different future toward which we are moving, which opens up an entirely different, new, and beautiful reality presently that we may live within. It is a reality that we embody and then open up for others.

It is a future that does not view the physical world as something from which people need to be "saved" or rescued at the last second and then taken to a spiritual heaven while everything we ever knew and loved about this beautiful life and creation is obliterated into smithereens by the fiery wrath of God.

Rather, it is a future in which the central purpose, the grand narrative, the overarching achievement of God is to bring heaven and earth lovingly and restoratively back together as one in perfect *shalom*. And that union and communion with the Divine, that wholeness and completeness and harmony with all things, that *shalom* with the Creator and all things, which will be fully and completely realized one day, begins in us right now.

The entire point of faith is to bring us into perfect and loving union with God, into a present shalom with the Divine and all things, in which we experience this life in all of its fullness, abundance, and beauty, and then take it with us as an invitation to all, so that they may too taste and see how good this life truly is.

That is precisely why Jesus said, "I have come that you would have life and have it in abundance, till it overflows."[6] He is not making some exclusive future promise about how good life will be in heaven one day. Jesus is saying that this life of abundance, this life of wholeness, completeness, and harmony in all things, this beautiful, wonderful life of *shalom* is here in the present, right here, right now. And it is here immersing you and washing over you and filling you until it overflows into everything you do. That is how we change our present and future, how we take light into the darkness, how we begin to make a difference in the social and cultural landscape of our country and world.

As we hope for a future of peace, we become that very peace now.

As we hope for a future of forgiveness, we become that very forgiveness now.

As we hope for a future of reconciliation, we become that very reconciliation now.

As we hope for a future of grace, we become that very grace now.

As we hope for a future of mercy, we become that very mercy now.

As we hope for a future of love, we become that very love now.

As we hope for a future of *shalom*, we become that very *shalom* now.

And that future is breaking mightily into our present, in and through our lives, in how we see, in how we relate, in how we serve, and in how we love.

Let heaven and earth be one,
And let it begin with us today.

PERFECT SHALOM OF THE CHRIST

The time in which we live is rich with opportunity for a new and better humanity that exists in perfect love and perfect freedom with God and with one another. And we are all invited out of the division and destruction and antipathy and hatred and fear that surrounds us, maybe even that in which we have participated, and into a uniting and edifying reality built upon goodness and love for all people that no longer sees the world as we versus they, but simply as we.

It is only in the perfect *shalom* of the Christ, through whom all the broken pieces of the universe—people and relationships and communities and all of creation—get repaired in perfect harmony.

It is only in the perfect *shalom* of the Christ that we can transcend polarization and avoid being easily blown to the extremes by the hateful litanies of propaganda, the perpetual rage of politics, and the we/they mudslinging.

It is only in the perfect *shalom* of the Christ where we no longer work divisively, or in ways that are antagonistic or counter-productive to peace. We do not take the side of one against another. We are peacemakers who work tirelessly for peace and forgiveness. It is only in the perfect *shalom* of the Christ where we no longer regard anyone from a worldly point of view, but from the point of view of God. Each person on earth has immeasurable worth and value because we are all in the Divine. To that end, we should see others as Christ sees them. We should treat others as Christ would treat them. We should speak of them as Christ would speak of them, as beloved brothers and sisters.

And to that end, we will love God and every single human being created in the image of God with our hearts, minds, and souls. And the way this love of God manifests in our lives is, not in guilting, shaming, wounding, hurting, devaluing, standing against, or damning another, but by a willingness to sacrifice one's self in order to demonstrate this radical love of God to another.

We will affirm the God-given worth and value of every single person on the planet from the time of their conception to their final breath of life, no matter their gender, gender identity, orientation, race, ethnicity, nationality, affiliation, ideology, religion, socio-economic status, citizenship status, or the sin in their life.

We will stand for and will actively work as peacemakers, not just in our own lives, but on behalf of every single life, every single relationship, every single community, and every single situation in which we find ourselves.

We will unambiguously and self-sacrificially stand, in solidarity and love with, by, and for every individual or group who is being marginalized, victimized, oppressed, harassed, terrorized, politicized, ostracized, or threatened, no matter who the aggressor may be, no matter if it is a person or a group with whom we may have previously aligned.

We will steadfastly respond in love to any and all verbal or physical antagonisms, threats, or offenses by another. For each person, even the most violent offender has immeasurable worth and value. Even more, a life fully rooted in the radical love of God can only respond in love, therefore we will respond to every verbal and physical aggression only in love.

We will work actively toward forgiveness and reconciliation, not just in our own lives, but between individuals and God, between individuals, and between people-groups, even when this means that we will likely loose standing or position from people or groups with whom we may have previously aligned, whether it be a religious or political or ideological group, for there is no other way forward in a hostile and divided world than in forgiveness and reconciliation.

We will strive for lives that emanate love, joy, peace, patience, kindness, goodness, faithfulness, gentleness, and self-control regardless of the changing conditions around us, regardless of how people, social media, the government, politicians, or the media may try to turn us against each other through propaganda and misinformation. We will choose to give others the benefit of a doubt and to love them despite what is said about them, even if it means standing against those with whom we previously aligned.

We will work tirelessly to invite every single person in the world out of systems, structures, organizations, and ideologies that work to divide and build antagonism between people through words and actions, whether it be political, governmental, religious, military, corporate, economic, or ideological, and into a new reality in which love is our absolute foundation, care and compassion is the means by which we relate to one another, grace and forgiveness and reconciliation is our modus operandi, peace is our undying disposition, and unity is the fabric of our relationships and communities.

AS SHALOM GOES FORTH

We can, and will, choose a different way in this hostile and divided world.

In every way our paths have been crooked, we look forward to a day when they are all made straight.

But as *shalom* goes forth, we begin straightening those paths today.

In every way that darkness surrounds and appears to prevail, we look forward to a day when the darkness will finally vanquish and Light will be victorious.

But as *shalom* goes forth, we begin today bearing this Light for all to see.

In every way the worth, value, and dignity of a person has been diminished for their color, gender, nationality, ethnicity, birthplace, socioeconomic level, disability, or sexual preference, we look forward to the day when we will fully and finally realize the profound worth and value that every single person has in the eyes of God since the creation of the world.

But as *shalom* goes forth, we begin today seeing people as God sees people, while fearlessly standing in solidarity against racism, bigotry, xenophobia, discrimination, and hatred and standing lovingly beside each person of the world.

In every way a human life has been devalued and terminated by our own hands, whether through unwanted pregnancies, capital punishment, violence, retribution, or war, we look forward to a day when the sting of death will subside, every tear will be wiped away, and our instruments of violence, war, and death will be no more.

But as *shalom* goes forth, we begin today working as humble, loving, nonjudgmental ambassadors of peace for all people, and between all people, for the common good, turning away from our instruments of violence, because we have an undying love for all people in every single relationship, in every single community, in every single nation, whether friend or enemy.

In every way that this good creation has been abused and exploited and injured, we look forward to a day when this creation will be renewed and restored and healed.

But as *shalom* goes forth, we begin today the work of stewarding and caretaking for the healing of this land and for the preservation of every single creature on earth.

In every way our relationships have been fractured and broken causing us to live in anger and distrust and resentment of one another, we look forward to a day of perfect harmony, unity, and community one with another and with God

But as *shalom* goes forth, we begin today preemptively working to heal the wounds, fractures, and divisions we have caused, seeking deeply rooted and intimate community in which we cooperate and share all that we have for the care and benefit of all.

In every way we have been suffocating in this busy life, missing the sacredness and presence of every moment, and missing the beauty in every detail of life, there will a day when we are fully awake and fully alive in every way.

But as *shalom* goes forth, we begin today praying with our every breath, receiving the grace and love of the Divine, while slowing our pace and awakening to the beauty that surrounds us, becoming fully present and alive in every moment.

In every way we have been led to believe that our sufferings should be cured once we have faith, there will be a day when the sufferings we have carried in this life journey will be fully and completely healed.

But as *shalom* goes forth, we will begin today carrying our sufferings together as a transformative passageway, while still standing in awe of the beauty and wonder and joy that exists in this life.

In every way we have believed that we can exist in this life isolated and separated from others, there will be a day when we are united in the brotherhood and sisterhood of all people.

But as *shalom* goes forth, we will begin to live in deeply rooted, nurturing relationships with our brothers and sisters of every gender, race, culture, religion, ethnicity, sexual preference, disability, and socioeconomic level.

IT STARTS WITH ME AND YOU

For the transformation we seek in this world does not begin on high in governments with rulers or leaders or politicians. It does not begin in the upper echelons of corporations or businesses with corporate executives. And it does not begin with charismatic preachers or with ordained ministers or at the highest levels of religious or denominational organization.

Rather, this transformation starts at the bottom with me and you as an organic, grassroots movement of *shalom*. And what begins as the smallest seeds of *shalom* planted in the fertile soil of our lives, quickly transforms into this deeply-rooted, intimately interconnected system that begins to move throughout every part of our communities and world. And this movement is never rooted in anger, violence, hatred, animosity, or vitriol, but in a peace and love that only comes from the nourishing *shalom* of God.

For what we seek is not an angry mob-rule, but a *shalom-filled* community of transformation.

And when we join together, this *shalom* begins to expose the darkness as it stands in stark and beautiful contrast to the power structures and systems of injustice, oppression, and violence.

Even as I write these words, there is a movement of those who follow Jesus coming together from across the nation in peace and love, extending *shalom* through word and action to press into the rising tide of Christian nationalism, hostilities against illegal immigrants and the breaking up of their families, misogyny and gender injustice, racial inequality and injustice, and poverty.

Even as I write these words, there is a movement of those who follow Jesus rising up as peacemakers to, not just stand in solidarity with the victims and families of students killed in more school shootings, but that is extending *shalom* through their peaceful call for legislative reform, through their peaceful activism of turning guns into gardening tools, and through offering a creative, prophetic vision for our country to reject violence and rediscover the peaceable non-violence of Jesus.

Even as I write these words, there is a movement of those who follow Jesus that are actively being the compassionate hands and feet of Christ, extending *shalom* by standing beside the LGBTQ community and pushing back against the hatred, antagonisms, and name-calling, and offering them a seat at the table as brothers and sisters, as they are continually pushed to the margins and ostracized by many Christians.

Even as I write these words, there is a movement of those who follow Jesus that are, not just helping those who are enslaved and chained to substance abuse and other addictions by meeting with them regularly, but also surrounding them in an honest, real, and vulnerable community that is deeply rooted and becoming more of a family that loves each other than a group that just gets together for meetings.

And this movement of *shalom* is moving and growing and expanding. The *shalom* of God is here and it is breaking into the present mightily. *Shalom* is not a passive, isolated state of being in oneself. It is an active, transformational, communal movement that is changing the world.

It is only peace that can stop the cycle of verbal and physical aggression.

It is only forgiveness that can stop the cycle of resentment and retaliation.

It is only reconciliation that can stop the cycle of fracturing and dividing.

It is only grace that can stop the cycle of judgment and condemnation.

It is only mercy that can stop the cycle of punishment and retribution.

It is only love that can stop the cycle of hatred and cover a multitude of offenses.

And it is only the *shalom* of God that will save us from ourselves. But this does not guarantee that *shalom* will be met with open arms. Far from it. The way of *shalom* may very well face the full frontal assault of evil and hatred, for the darkness despises the light. But it is this self-sacrificing, other-centered, friend-and-enemy-loving *shalom* that is the embodiment of the Christ in the world that will win in the end. So we fearlessly, courageously, and hopefully carry this light of *shalom* in the darkness presently for the world to see.

There is a different way to live this life. And it is here and it is going forth.

This faith is not about doing something in the future, while ignoring the present as inconsequential. This present life matters right now, and extending the ever-present *shalom* of God in our lives, our families, our relationship, our communities, and in the world, is worth dying for. Because that is where perfect freedom and perfect love is embodied. It is where our deepest longings, our deepest desires are realized. It is where union and communion with the Divine extends outward through our lives. It is where we discover the wholeness, completeness, and harmony of all things and where we learn to see beauty, we learn to be beauty, in the middle of the wreckage of this life.

QUESTIONS

1. As we have neglected the pursuit of *shalom* in our lives, relationships, and communities, what has been the impact on each?

2. What are the consequences of simply becoming the same brokenness that we face each day?

3. How is *shalom* intrinsically connected to justice and righteousness?

4. As one you begin to pursue a life of *shalom*, what is one concrete step you can take to in your community and in your world, as it relates to efforts of restorative justice, peace, forgiveness, reconciliation, human dignity and equality, and leading others into the ways of *shalom*?

5. What does it look like for you to be an ambassador of *shalom* in your family, among your friends, in your neighborhoods, in your schools, in your community, and in the global community?

A Litany of Hope

Where O Light are you in this darkness? Give us hope. We are drowning in the nightfall that surrounds us. We are shrouded and enveloped by the dark cloud cover. We are walking in shadows and grasping for walls as blind leading the blind. Night, my God, it threatens to devour and swallow us whole.

Where O Light are you in this darkness? Give us hope.

For we fear this darkness will not pass. We fear this is the way life will always be. We fear that death will pronounce our final verdict and declaration. Night, my God, it threatens to devour and swallow us whole.

Where O Light are you in this darkness? Give us hope.

Our hearts are crushed and broken. Our sufferings are excruciating and immeasurable. Our tears continue to fall but they do not console. Night, my God, it threatens to devour and swallow us whole.

Where O Light are you in this darkness? Give us hope.

Give us hope this darkness will pass. Give us hope life will not always be this way. Give us hope that death will not be the final victor. Night, my God, it threatens to devour and swallow us whole.

Where O Light are you in this darkness? Give us hope.

Light of forgiveness and grace break through. Light of justice and mercy prevail. Light of love illuminate. Day, my God, may it break and make us whole.

Where O light are you in this darkness?

Where O light are you in this darkness?

Where O light are you in this darkness?

Give us hope.

The Light of Christ is breaking in beautifully and victoriously. But the Light of Christ, continues in you.

We will be the light that pushes back when nightfall surrounds us. We will be the light that overcomes when shrouded and enveloped by the dark cloud cover. We will be the light that exposes the shadows so that all may see clearly the paths of righteousness. Day, my God, is breaking. Make us whole.

We will be the light in the darkness. Hope is in this place.

We will not fear and this darkness will pass. We will not fear because life will not be overtaken. We will not fear death because this is not our final verdict or declaration. Day, my God, is breaking. Make us whole.

We will be the light in the darkness. Hope is in this place.

We will carry each other until our hearts are healed and restored. We will embrace each other until our sufferings are stories of victory. We will hold each other until our tears are wiped away and all is made right. Day, my God, is breaking. Make us whole.

We will be the light in the darkness. Hope is in this place.

Let us be hope each day until this darkness passes. Let us give hope that life does not always be this way. Let us shout and proclaim our hope and that death is not the final victor. Day, my God, is breaking. Make us whole.

We will be the light in the darkness. Hope is in this place.

For we are the light of forgiveness and grace that is breaking through. For we are the light of justice and mercy that is prevailing. For we are the light of love that is illuminating. Day, my God, is breaking. Let us bring *shalom* to your people and to your land.

We are the Light in the darkness. We are the Body of hope. Amen.

Endnotes

CHAPTER 2

1. Galatians 3:28 and Colossians 3:11

2. John 2:1-11

CHAPTER 3

1. Matthew 23:13 NIV

2. Matthew 13:44

3. Lawrence, Brother Lawrence, *His Conversations and Letters on the Practice of the Presence of God*. Cincinnati, Ohio: Forward Movement Publications, 1960. Print.

4. Matthew 7:13-14 NIV

5. John 3:1-21

6. *HELPS* word studies (Gary Hill)

7. Romans 3:23

8. 2 Corinthians 5: 11-21

9. *HELPS* word studies (Gary Hill)

10. Matthew 19:24

11. Philippians 4:1-13 AMP

CHAPTER 4

1. Romans 5:3-4 NIV

CHAPTER 5

1. Romans 8: 22-28 AMP

2. Romans 8:26

CHAPTER 6

1. Ephesians 6:18

2. *HELPS* word studies (Gary Hill)

CHAPTER 7

1. John 15:5 MSG

2. Matthew 13

3. Matthew 13:10 NIV

4. Myers, Kelly A. *Metanoia and the Transformation of Opportunity.* Rhetoric Society Quarterly, Vol. 41, No. 1, pp. 1–18.

5. Romans 2:4

CHAPTER 8

1. Rohr, Richard. *Everything Belongs.* The Crossroad Publishing Company. 2003, March.

2. Isaiah 55:12 NIV

CHAPTER 9

1. McEwen, Annie, and Farrell, Brenna, Producers. "From Tree to Shining Tree." *Radiolab*, WNYC Studios, 30 July 2016.

2. Matthew 5:23-24

3. Romans 12:18

4. Matthew 12:48 NIV

5. Colossians 3:15

CHAPTER 10

1. Plato. *Plato's The Republic*. New York :Books, Inc., 1943. Print.

2. 1 John 4:18

3. King, Martin Luther. *Strength to Love*, New York : Harper & Row, ©1963.

4. John 4:32

5. John 14:27. The word *peace* is the Greek word *eiréné* and its Hebrew equivalent is *shalom*.

6. John 10:10 AMP

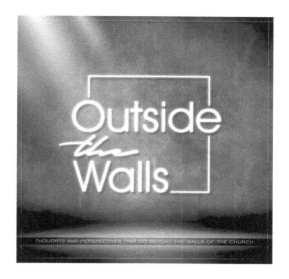

Outside the Walls is the creative expression of Brandon Andress, Sarah Lowry Dismore, and Jess Duncan, focusing on Jesus and the Kingdom of God and how we can become extensions of that reality into our culture and throughout the world, no matter how taboo the topic may be.

For more information about Brandon Andress
or to contact him for speaking engagements,
please visit *www.BrandonAndress.com*

Many voices. One message.

Quoir is a boutique publisher
with a singular message: *Christ is all.*
Venture beyond your boundaries to discover Christ
in ways you never thought possible.

For more information, please visit
www.quoir.com

CPSIA information can be obtained
at www.ICGtesting.com
Printed in the USA
LVHW091458011121
702129LV00016B/723